ESSENTIAL
BULBS

ESSENTIAL
BULBS

The 100 Best for Design and Cultivation

Text and Photography by Derek Fell

B. Mitchell

A FRIEDMAN GROUP BOOK

Copyright © 1989 by Michael Friedman Publishing Group, Inc.

ISBN 0-88665-600-1

ESSENTIAL BULBS: The 100 Best for Design and Cultivation
was prepared and produced by
Michael Friedman Publishing Group, Inc.
15 West 26th Street
New York, NY 10010

Editor: Sharon Kalman
Art Director/Designer: Robert W. Kosturko
Photography Editor: Christopher Bain
Production Manager: Karen L. Greenberg
Layout/Illustrations: Alanna M. Georgens

Typeset by Mar+x Myles Graphics, Inc.
Color separated, printed, and bound by South Sea International Press, Ltd.

h g f e d c b a

ACKNOWLEDGMENTS

The author wishes to thank the many expert bulb gardeners who gave him free access
to their gardens, especially Charles H. Mueller, bulb specialist, of
New Hope, Pennsylvania and Robert L. Greene who has created a magnificent,
naturalistic bulb garden at Tollgate Farm, Pennsylvania.
Also, a special thanks to the staff of The Netherlands Flower Bulb Institute for providing
help in locating many photogenic bulb displays and flower fields during a productive
five-day visit to Holland at the height of the spring-flowering season.

TABLE OF CONTENTS

9   **INTRODUCTION**

A BIG BANG FOR THE BUCK
HISTORY OF BULB GROWING

13   **CHAPTER ONE**

BULB BASICS
WHEN TO PLANT
HOW TO NATURALIZE SPRING-FLOWERING BULBS
GROWING BULBS INDOORS
GROWING BULBS OUTDOORS

27   **CHAPTER TWO**

THE ENCYCLOPEDIA OF ESSENTIAL BULBS

97   **CHAPTER THREE**

GARDEN PLANS
ISLAND BED OF SUMMER-FLOWERING BULBS
INFORMAL BULB BORDER

FORMAL BULB GARDEN
WINTER-FLOWERING BULB GARDEN
ISLAND BED OF FALL-FLOWERING BULBS
FORMAL PARTERRE GARDEN OF SPRING-FLOWERING BULBS
WINTER GARDEN FEATURING SPRING AND SUMMER BULBS
FREE-FORM BED OF SPRING-AND SUMMER-FLOWERING BULBS
CUTTING GARDEN FOR SPRING AND SUMMER BULBS
ROCK GARDEN FOR SPRING-FLOWERING BULBS

119   CHAPTER FOUR

PLANT SELECTION GUIDE

128   APPENDIX I
   BULB PLANTING CHARTS

134   APPENDIX II
   BULB FLOWERING GUIDE

140   SOURCES

142   INDEX OF BOTANICAL AND COMMON NAMES

Yellow, orange, pink, and red tulips and grape hyacinths are displayed here on a hillside at the famous Keukenhoff Bulb Garden, Lisse, Holland.

INTRODUCTION

A BIG BANG FOR THE BUCK

IT IS DIFFICULT TO HAVE A SATISFYING ORNAmental garden without taking advantage of the wide variety of flowering bulbs. Many bulbs have the color impact of annuals *and* the staying power of perennials. In addition to coming back year after year, many hardy types can survive arcticlike winters, while tender varieties will survive long periods of drought.

Bulbs can establish a garden's reputation like few other plant groups. At Keukenhoff, in Holland, displays of spring-flowering bulbs attract thousands of visitors from all over the world each year. In North America, at the estate garden of Winterthur (Delaware), the late Henry F. du Pont planted bulbs in vast quantities across meadows and among woodland. Hundreds of thousands of daffodils, bluebells, lilies, and colchicums were planted so thickly that du Pont literally painted the landscape with flowering bulbs, much like an artist daubing paint on a canvas.

Of course, gardeners do not need hundreds of acres or thousands of a single variety to enjoy the beauty of flowering bulbs. As few as fifteen bulbs clustered together can create a bold splash of color in a small bed or border.

The varieties presented here represent the best bulbs for today's gardens. Many are hardy and will grow in most of the colder regions of Canada. Others are tender. In the northern United States tender bulbs can be planted outdoors in the spring to flower in summer or fall. They must, however, be lifted from the ground soon after frost kills the top growth and be stored in a cool, frost-free basement over winter. In areas of the country with mild winters, such as the Gulf States, the Southwest, and California, many tender varieties can be grown outdoors year-round.

Bulbs serve many different purposes. Some are good for naturalizing, multiplying year after year; others make beautiful houseplants when grown in pots. An important section of this book presents useful lists and charts—grouping plants by color, height, bloom period, and other designations.

In addition, there is an unique design section presenting garden plans for different situations—island beds, shady borders, rock gardens, and cutting gardens, for example. These plans are easily adapted to individual preferences and site restrictions.

The plant section features 100 entries, each describing the characteristics of the plant and its cultural needs. In most cases the accompanying photograph shows each plant *in situ*, so the gardener can gain a clear idea of what the plant looks like in a garden setting.

Finally, *Essential Bulbs* closes with a list of sources, including general bulb suppliers who sell a wide assortment of bulbs as well as bulb specialists who sometimes offer over 1,000 varieties of a particular bulb group—turn to them when you want to build a bulb collection or seek the rare and unusual.

The big attraction to bulbs among home gardeners is the ease with which they can be planted and the high probability that they will flower the following season without a lot of care. Even the smallest bulbs, such as snowdrops and aconites, are larger than most bean seeds and contain enough stored energy within their fleshy interiors to propel themselves into full flower with the merest covering of soil and moisture. With larger bulbs, such as daffodils and tulips, the task of planting is even easier. Simply stated, bulbs are a gardener's dream come true: a big bang for the buck with a minimum of effort.

Right: Hortus Bulborum Bulb Garden at Limmen, Holland is a display garden planted with old varieties and species of bulbs, some dating as far back as the 1500s.

Far right: The triumph tulip, Kees Nelis, in the Hortus Bulborum display garden.

Opposite page: Tulip fields in northern Holland. After the bulbs flower, the growers evaluate the quality of the crop, then chop off all but one of the blooms so that the plant's energy is directed at growing a single, large bulb.

HISTORY OF BULB GROWING

Primitive civilizations first valued bulbs for food and medicine. Though many are poisonous—such as daffodils and hyacinths—a large number are edible either raw (onions), cooked (dahlia tubers), or pounded into a pasty substance (elephant ears or "taro"—a source of poi, the Polynesian food staple). The autumn-flowering saffron crocus yields golden yellow, powdery stigmas and has been cultivated for centuries as a valuable source of flavoring and dye. Evidence of its early use appears on a jar from the island of Crete, dating to 1500 B.C. Colchicums yield a valuable medicinal substance called *colchicine*. The rhizome of an iris produces *orris* used in cosmetics as a scent, and North American Indians fiercely guarded tribal rights to vast meadows of *camassias* whose bulbs were a vital food.

The first mention of using bulbs in gardens appears in the writings of Theophrastus, a Greek philosopher, who lived around 300 B.C. In his book, *A History of Plants and Theoretical Botany,* he describes anemones, crocus, gladiolus, grape hyacinths, lilies, and ranunculus. Dioscorides, a Greek physician, and Pliny, a Roman scholar, further describe alliums, daffodils, hyacinths, and scillas.

By the mid-sixteenth century, tulips had found their way into Austrian gardens through trade with Turkey. Carolus Clusias, curator of Emperor Maximillian the Second's medicinal garden, collected many unusual flowering bulbs, including the tulip. When he lost his position after the Emperor's death in 1576, he emigrated to Holland, taking with him a large assortment of plants, including tulips. He was appointed curator of the Hortus Medicus medicinal garden in Leyden. The tulips he planted there aroused great interest among the Dutch. The flowers were so richly colored,

everyone wanted to grow them. Moreover, the tulip had an inherent tendency to produce color mutations—sometimes in solid colors, but also streaked with a contrasting color.

When a tulip produced a distinctive mutation, it could be further propagated from bulblets. First, the wealthy classes wanted new tulip varieties to grow in their gardens, and then the masses became obsessed with growing them. Speculators paid huge prices for a single bulb of a new variety if they thought it would generate a popular following. During the early seventeenth century tulips could be traded like stocks, and they changed hands by the cartload. The crash came suddenly in 1637 when public demand waned. Investors found themselves stuck with bulbs that could fetch only 5 percent of the purchase price, and political cartoonists delighted in portraying tulip traders as baboons.

In spite of their tarnished image, tulips continued to be produced in Holland by a core of growers who specialized in the breeding, propagating, and exporting of bulbs. The cool climate and sandy soil were perfect for growing tulips, and to this day Holland has remained the preeminent breeder and producer of tulips.

Holland also produces vast quantities of daffodils, hyacinths, and "minor bulbs" such as iris, grape hyacinths, aconites, and crocus; however, several other nations compete with Holland. In North America, the Pacific Northwest possesses ideal conditions for breeding and producing daffodils, dahlias, and lilies. Parts of Michigan have proven especially favorable for daylilies. Scotland, Ireland, and England all actively breed and produce daffodils and dahlias. Some Japanese growers have become expert producers of tulips and irises.

For the American gardener, bulbs are readily available from a multitude of local sources. Garden centers offer selections of popular varieties: summer-flowering bulbs on sale in spring for spring planting and spring-flowering bulbs on sale in fall for fall planting. A larger selection is available from catalog houses, a list of which is featured at the back of this book. Traditionally, mail-order bulb suppliers have published their bulb catalogs in summer to give gardeners ample time to order for fall planting. However, several companies now publish their bulb catalogs in spring and offer substantial "pre-season" discounts for early orders.

CHAPTER ONE

BULB BASICS

THE BULB IS ONE OF NATURE'S INGENIOUS inventions. It enables the plants to lie dormant, withstanding long periods of harsh conditions (usually severe temperatures or dry summers) until the plants bloom again. Generally, a bulb is an enlarged portion of root or stem comprised of a storehouse of energy that is released when certain favorable conditions cause it to break dormancy. It then sprouts leaves, produces flowers, sets seeds, and grows bulblets, ensuring a new generation of the plant. The favorable conditions that are needed to break dormancy are generally a combination of moisture, sunlight, and warm temperatures.

Some bulbs are extremely hardy, withstanding severe frosts; others are tender and are killed by freezing temperatures. Most bulbs require good drainage to survive from year to year, but a few, such as calla lilies, will tolerate permanently moist soil. Bulbs include spring-flowering, summer-flowering, and autumn-flowering kinds. Many can be flowered indoors or under glass during winter months by a special "forcing" technique (see page 19).

True Bulbs, such as tulips and daffodils, are essentially underground "buds" formed by a swollen portion of stem. Each bulb has a growing point and is composed of fleshy layers, like an onion. The layers are wrapped around the growing point, as with tulips, or the layers are composed of scales, as with lilies. At the bottom of true bulbs is a disk from which roots emerge. Bulbs also produce bulblets, which can produce a new plant.

Corms, such as crocus and gladiolus, are solid. As the food supply in the corm is used up it shrivels away and is replaced by a new corm that forms on the top of the old one. Like bulbs, corms have a basal disk from which roots emerge. Corms also produce cormlets.

Tubers, such as dahlias and caladiums, are similar to corms in that they are solid. They can be stem tubers, like caladiums, or root tubers, like dahlias. Neither has a basal disk, but are covered with "eyes," which are buds on the surface of the tuber or concentrated near the stem section.

Rhizomes, such as irises and calla lilies, are horizontal sections of swollen stem that lie on or below the ground. Buds on top of the rhizome produce new green growth, while roots develop along the underside.

One of the advantages of using bulbs, corms, tubers, and rhizomes is that they are large and easy to handle compared to other means of reproduction, such as seeds and cuttings. Bulbs also are easily planted, dependable, and capable of producing a bold splash of color quite quickly. Because of their similarities, most garden supply houses classify bulbs, corms, tubers, and rhizomes simply as "bulbs."

By their nature, all bulbs—corms, tubers, and rhizomes—are "perennials." If their cultural needs are met, they will come up faithfully year after year. Also, like most garden perennials, their floral display can be short-lived, although there are exceptions, such as tuberous begonias and dahlias.

A careful selection of bulbs can provide nine months of color, starting with aconites and snowdrops that bloom in early spring and ending with autumn-flowering crocus.

WHEN TO PLANT

Most bulbs can be categorized by their flowering period. When and how to plant these bulbs depends solely on when they flower. See the encyclopedia chapter for more detailed planting information for each bulb. In order to ensure a long bloom period throughout the season, plant a good mixture of spring-, summer-, and fall-flowering bulbs.

Spring-Flowering Bulbs

Plant the bulbs when the soil cools to below 60° F (15°C). In northern regions, plant in either late September or early October.

In warm climates, store the bulbs in an open container in the vegetable compartment of your refrigerator for six to eight weeks before planting. Don't place the bulbs next to fruit such as tomatoes, apples, or pears, since these give off a gas harmful to bulbs. This cold period simulates the chilling they would normally receive in the ground. Plant the bulbs on a cool day in late November or December.

Summer- and Fall-Flowering Bulbs

Plant the bulbs in spring when the danger of heavy frosts is past. Generally, in northern regions summer-flowering bulbs can be planted as late as the beginning of June. Fall-flowering bulbs are best planted before the end of June. Many of them produce leaves that die before the plants flower.

HOW TO NATURALIZE SPRING-FLOWERING BULBS

Perhaps nothing is more symbolic of spring than a sunny slope full of daffodils tossing their golden trumpets in the wind. Many spring-flowering bulbs, such as daffodils, will give a good show the first flowering season, but will flower progressively less in subsequent years until they completely peter out. Unfortunately, there is more to naturalizing a landscape than popping bulbs into the ground and hoping they will take care of themselves.

In most cases where bulbs fail to naturalize, the problem is poor feeding. With most flowering bulbs the most essential fertilizer nutrient is phosphorous. This is why experts recommend bone meal—phosphorous-rich fertilizer—for fall plantings. However, for naturalized plantings bone meal can be prohibitively expensive. Super phosphate provides a more economical substitute. (For more details on fertilizing, see page 22.)

Where soils are deficient in phosphorous, try two applications (one in the spring—before the bulbs flower—and one in the fall) of super phosphate mixed with a soil conditioner such as compost, dehydrated manure, peat moss, or leaf mold. Combine these two basic ingredients at the ratio of 1 to 1 by weight and apply 10 pounds of the mixture per 100 bulbs.

The daffodil is without doubt the most dependable bulb for naturalizing wherever cold winter temperatures can be relied on to provide a dormant period. Best of all, the bulbs are large and easy to handle. They will naturalize in open, sunny locations such as meadows, as well as in lightly shaded areas such as under deciduous trees. More importantly, daffodil bulbs are poisonous to rodents, who are notoriously destructive to naturalized plantings.

Classic naturalized settings for daffodils include areas alongside a sparkling stream, at the edge of a pond, on a sunny bank, or clustered around a clump of silver birch on an open lawn. To gain a naturalized effect, you can choose the less expensive bulb mixtures, and some catalogs will even feature a "naturalized collection" at a special low rate.

SPRING-FLOWERING BULBS SUITABLE FOR NATURALIZING

*Asterisked varieties are tender

VARIETY	LOCATION
Amaryllis belladonna	Sun, meadow
Camassia	Sun, meadow
Chionodoxa	Sun or shade, rock garden, woodland
Clivia miniata	Shade
Crocus	Sun or shade, lawn or meadow
Eranthis	Sun or shade, woodland
Erythronium	Sun or shade, rock garden
Fritillaria imperialis	Sun or shade, edge of woodland
Galanthus	Sun or shade, woodland, rock garden
Hyacinthoides	Shade, woodland
Iris cristata	Sun or shade, woodland
Iris reticulata	Sun, rock garden
Muscari	Sun or shade, rock garden
Narcissus	Sun or shade, woodland, meadow, lawn
Ornithogalum species	Sun, meadow, rock garden
Oxalis species	Sun, meadow
Tulipa species	Sun or shade, rock garden
Zephyranthes atamasco	Sun or shade, woodland, meadow

When planting, it is best to gently scatter the bulbs on the ground, and plant them where they fall. Leaf mold, peat moss, or well-decomposed animal manure and garden compost scattered onto the surface of the garden in the fall will work its way into the subsoil and benefit the bulb plantings.

Never mow a naturalized area until the leaves of the plantings have completely died away, since the leaves enable the new season's bulb to properly mature and multiply. Good drainage, of course, is essential to avoid waterlogging, which will rot the bulbs.

Some of the most effective daffodils for naturalizing include the dainty Hoop Petticoat *(Narcissus bulbocodium)*; miniature daffodils *(Narcissus minimum)* such as Dove Wings and February Gold; the Poeticus class, such as Pheasant's Eye and Actaea; and the large trumpet daffodils *(Narcissus hybrida* 'Trumpet-flowered'), King Alfred (all yellow), Music Hall (white petals, yellow trumpet), and Beersheba (all white). These are all old-fashioned varieties, but thoroughly dependable, still widely available, and relatively inexpensive for naturalizing when planted in color groups.

Planting depths for daffodils vary according to the size of the bulb, but for the giant trumpet daffodils, six inches, measuring from the tip of the bulb, is about right. Recommended spacing is six inches apart. (For more spring-flowering bulbs suitable for naturalizing, see page 15.)

You must be more selective when choosing varieties of tulips for naturalizing, since the majority of varieties in catalogs will not naturalize, and those that do will not normally naturalize through sod. For tulips, a rock garden is ideal.

Another problem with tulips is their susceptibility to rodent damage. Even chipmunks and squirrels will search them out and destroy a new planting even before it has time to flower in the first season. Planting rodent repellent flakes helps protect the bulbs through the first season. Once the bulbs are established, rodent damage is usually not so great. Outdoor cats also provide effective control against rodents.

For smaller naturalized areas the *kaufmanniana* (or water-lily) tulips are dependable; also tulip species *chrysantha, turkestanica, sylvestris, dasystemons* and *clusiana.* The *kaufmannianas* are the earliest to bloom, opening their petals out flat when the sun shines, just like a water lily. *Clusiana* resembles a miniature candlestick tulip, since it holds its red

and white striped petals upright. The *dasystemon* has a beautiful star shape, flowering close to the ground, with a distinctive yellow center and white petal edge.

In the rock garden, these species of tulips are effective when planted among rocky outcrops and dwarf conifers; however, the soil should be mulched with some natural-looking fibrous material to keep down the weeds.

Crocus are a favorite for naturalizing in a lawn. For extra-early blooms, choose yellow, and for largest size, choose purple varieties. Mixtures, of course, are effective and less expensive than buying separate colors, but once you have seen a lawn planted exclusively with bright yellow crocus or the striped Pickwick, you will realize how effective and well worth the extra cost a single-color planting can be.

To naturalize crocus in a lawn it is best to remove areas of sod, plant the bulbs two inches into the bare soil, and replace the sod after planting. This is generally easier and more effective than trying to plant the small bulbs through the grass with a trowel or bulb planter. By repeating this procedure in several areas, you will soon have beautiful, naturalized patches. Remember to feed twice a year and never mow until the spiky leaves have withered. Rodents consider crocus an extra tasty tidbit—rabbits will eat the tops—so where these pests present a potential problem, it is sometimes better to stick to the more dependable daffodil for naturalizing.

Winter aconite is a very dependable bulb for naturalizing. It is a good companion to snowdrops in a naturalized landscape, since the two bloom at about the same time—the yellow aconite contrasting with the pure white snowdrops. These two grow especially well at the edge of lightly wooded areas, where plenty of leaf mold enriches the soil.

Siberian squill, grape hyacinth, snow crocus, and *chionodoxa* will brighten up similar locations. A rock garden where they can be planted in thick clumps or bold drifts among boulders and driftwood is also a perfect place for these charming beauties.

GROWING BULBS INDOORS

There is a special pleasure in having rooms in the house filled with the color and fragrance of flowering bulbs, especially during winter months when the world outdoors is bleak and cold. The most popular varieties for fragrance are hyacinths and paperwhites, which can be forced into bloom using water alone. For sheer color impact, nothing can outshine the spectacular giant-flowering amaryllis, grown in a pot with soil. Tulips, daffodils, crocus, and grape hyacinths are also easily forced into early bloom in a pot of soil. Some varieties are easier to force than others, and usually the label on a bulb package (or the catalog description) will tell you which varieties are recommended and how to do the forcing.

Some bulbs need a "precooling" treatment in order to bloom indoors. Hyacinths, tulips, and daffodils, for example, generally need twelve weeks at 45° F or cooler in a dark place before transferring them to a room environment. To achieve this, place the bulbs in an unheated basement, a cold frame, or bury them in a trench in the ground. Cover the pots with an insulating material such as straw or pine bark, and check on them periodically to be sure they are moist but not soaked in water.

In warmer climates, refrigerate the bulbs. It is best to first plant them in a pot and refrigerate the whole package. If you don't have room for this, refrigerate just the bulbs in an open container for twelve weeks. Then pot them and place the pots in the coolest place you have while the roots grow—perhaps in a garage, utility room, or closet.

Mark your calendar when you begin cooling the bulbs so you will know when it is time to move them out into the light. By the end of the cooling period, shoots will appear. If you potted many bulbs and want them to flower over a period of time, remove them one at a time over several weeks.

Potting the Bulbs

Hyacinths are often grown in a specially shaped hyacinth glass that holds the bulb just above the water, with plenty of room for the roots to grow. Everyone seems to enjoy watching the white roots grow inside the crystal glass, finally leading up to a cluster of fragrant flowers.

Hyacinths and paperwhites can also be grown in a dish of pebbles (used for support) with water in the bottom. Any sort of container that holds water will do, but a low, shallow dish is best. A clear container will help you check the water level and

Opposite page: A crocus corm in flower, uprooted to show the structure of the entire plant.
Above left: An amaryllis bulb planted in a plastic pot. After watering, the bulb will sprout and bloom within three weeks.
Below left: A group of three paperwhite narcissus bulbs planted in a special pot that suspends them above the water, allowing the roots to drink but the bulbs to remain dry.

the progress of the roots. It is important to keep the water level just below the bulb base. Any lower and the roots may dry out, any higher and the bulb may rot. A little charcoal in the container keeps the water clean.

Paperwhites do not need a cooling period. They need only to be potted and then put in the sun, and they'll bloom in three to five weeks.

Most bulbs, including hyacinths and paperwhites, are best grown in a pot with soil. Either plastic or clay pots will do, but the container must have a drainage hole in the bottom. The shape of the pot is not critical, but a low bulb pan provides a sturdy shape for growing a group of tall flowers.

Plant the bulbs in a commercial potting soil or a mixture of one part peat, one part perlite, and one part garden soil. (Garden soil alone will pack down too hard in the pot and should not be used.)

Be generous with the number of bulbs you put in each pot; however, avoid crowding the flowers. In a six-inch pot you can plant three hyacinths, six tulips, five daffodils, or twelve crocus bulbs. When planting tulips, place the flat side toward

the edge of the pot so the large first leaf will grow outward over the edge. Plant the bulbs deep enough so that only their tips are above the soil and water them thoroughly after planting. (Of course, if you were planting these bulbs outside in the garden you would plant them much deeper and farther apart. See page 21.)

Flowering on a Sunny Windowsill

For shoot and flower development, bulbs need bright light. Place them in a south or west window or on a sun porch. In mild climates, put them outside in the sun. Temperatures should range from 55° to 65°F (12° to 18° C). Growth is rapid from this point, and flower buds will soon emerge. Then place the flowers wherever they will be enjoyed most. They will last longer if temperatures are on the cool side.

Bulbs that have been forced will not likely bloom the next year, and it is best to discard them when the blooms fade. If you wish, you can plant them in an out of the way spot in the garden.

Amaryllis

The amaryllis is a popular house plant for indoor growing because of its big, bold flowers and ease of culture. It is a tropical plant that needs only a slight cooling period. Just plant the bulb in a six-inch pot with potting soil so that the top third of the bulb is above the soil line. To start amaryllis, place the pot in a warm location (70° to 75°F [21° to 24°C]) until the flowers begin to color. Watering should be light at first. After the flower stalk is one inch tall, water it enough to keep the soil moist but not soggy. When the bulbs flower, put the pot in a cool place to prolong the life of the flower.

To rejuvenate an amaryllis after it has flowered, keep the bulb indoors in its pot until the danger of frost is past. Keep the long, green leaves healthy for as long as possible by continuing to water. Then transfer the bulb outdoors to a shady part of the garden with fertile soil. Usually the leaves will remain green until fall frost, at which time the bulb should be lifted and stored for a minimum of ten weeks in a cool basement. After this period of cold treatment, the bulb can then be potted, brought into the light, and watered to reflower.

GROWING BULBS OUTDOORS

First loosen the soil by digging at least eight inches below the eventual depth of the bulbs. Mix in some lime and organic matter to improve the soil as needed. Lime lowers the pH in acidic soil, while organic matter improves clay or sandy soil. For bigger, more vigorous blooms, fertilize the area with a high-phosphorus fertilizer, such as Bulb Booster, according to the directions on the bag. Bulb Booster is made especially for bulbs and releases plant nutrients at just the right times in the bulb's growth cycle.

Plant the bulbs with the pointed end up—large bulbs about eight inches deep, small bulbs about five inches deep. Space the bulbs far enough apart so that the flowers will not be

Left: The Queen of Sheba, a lily-flowered tulip, makes an attractive border at the edge of a lawn.

crowded, but close enough that the planting will look full. (See the individual plant descriptions for suggested planting depths and spacing.)

After preparing the soil, use a bulb planter or trowel to dig individual holes for each bulb. For even flowering, be sure all the bulbs of the same kind are at the same depth.

After planting, water thoroughly and place three inches of mulch over the bed to deter weeds and to provide winter protection for fall-planted bulbs.

The bulbs continue to grow after blooming, storing food and forming next year's flowers. Good care at this time is very important for vigorous blooms the following spring. Remove the dead flowers so the bulbs won't use energy making seeds. Allow the foliage to yellow and wither naturally. Never cut the leaves off until they are completely brown. Leave the bulbs in the ground through the summer and fertilize again in fall.

For naturalized plantings it is important to get an informal look. To do this, mark out the area you want to plant with flour, lime, or string, and gently scatter the bulbs onto the ground, planting them where they fall. If bulbs are planted through sod, it is important to fertilize them twice a year so they remain sufficiently vigorous and can compete with the grass and grow through the sod. Fertilize in spring before the bulbs bloom, and again in fall.

Fertilizing Bulbs

To keep bulbs healthy and coming back each year, feeding is essential. The most important plant nutrients are nitrogen, phosphorus, and potash. Because they are essential to the healthy development of cultivated plants, all fertilizer formulas by law must show the percentage of each major nutrient. These are expressed in a nitrogen-phosphorus-potash ratio, such as 5-10-5 or 10-20-10. In a 5-10-5 formula, a total of 20 percent is active nutrient; the rest is "filler" that acts as a distributing agent. This is helpful to know when deciding comparative values, since a one pound package of 5-10-5 (twenty percent total nutrient content) at the same price as a one pound package of 10-20-10 (forty percent) would not be as good a buy. Phosphorus is the most important ingredient since it is responsible for healthy root and bulb development.

For outdoor bulb plantings it is best to feed bulbs twice a year—in autumn after planting and again in spring before they bloom. If you only have time to feed them once a year do it after planting, in autumn, and again the following year in early autumn. For summer-flowering bulbs, feed in spring.

For the best results, sprinkle the fertilizer on the soil surface and rake it into the topsoil at the rate recommended on the label. (For special instructions concerning naturalized plantings, see page 14.)

Composting can also supply food for bulb plantings, eliminating the need for packaged fertilizer. However, unless properly made, garden compost may supply too much nitrogen, causing leaves to develop at the expense of flowers. If compost is made mostly from decomposed animal manure, kitchen and garden waste, lawn clippings, sawdust, shredded leaves, and similar materials, then bone meal or superphosphate (high-phosphorus ingredients) should be mixed in at the time of application.

Soil Conditioning

Soil can be classified as clay, loam, or sand. Clay is heavy, cold, and forms a sticky mass when it is squeezed. It is impervious to water, which "puddles" on the surface. Sand—at the other extreme—is granular, doesn't bind together when squeezed, has poor moisture-holding capacity, and allows nutrients to drain quickly. Loam is a balanced mixture of clay, sand, and organic matter. The addition of organic matter will improve both clay and sandy soil. You will not improve sand by adding clay, nor improve clay by adding sand. Only the introduction of organic material—with its fluffy texture and aeration qualities—will break down clay or add body to sand.

Opposite page: At the Presby Iris Garden, near Montclair, New Jersey, hybrids of *Iris germanica* (bearded iris) create a rainbow border. *Left:* Clumps of Siberian iris foliage changing color in the fall. The rhizomes remain dormant in the soil throughout the winter and prior to flowering, sprout fresh green leaves in the spring.

Right: To create leaf mold, fallen leaves can be stored in an enclosure of chicken wire and left to decompose.

The Value of Leaf Mold

Leaf mold, the product of leaf litter, is the most important soil conditioner for improving the growth of bulbs. It can be found in both deciduous and evergreen wooded areas under the surface layer of dried fallen leaves. It is usually black or dark brown in color, fluffy in texture, and rich in nutrients—particularly trace elements. Moreover, its moisture-holding capacity is enormous—up to ten times better than unimproved garden topsoil.

The best way to obtain leaf mold is to create a leaf pile using chicken wire to form a holding area. Small leaves, such as pine needles and willow leaves, can be piled into the bin as they are collected, but larger leaves, such as oak and maple, need to be shredded first, either by using a leaf shredder or a lawn mower.

Shredded leaves not only take up less volume than unshredded leaves, but also decompose much faster. Unshredded leaves can take a year or more to decompose, while shredded leaves can be useable as leaf mold within several months, particularly in warm weather and if an "activator" is mixed into the pile. An activator is any source of nitrogen. Nitrogen occurs naturally in green plant material, such as grass clippings, as well as blood meal, animal manure, and greensand. Packaged activators are also available from garden centers.

Leaf mold should be applied to bulb beds in spring after the plants bloom and then again in autumn. Either spread it on top of the soil as a mulch or rake it into the upper soil surface.

Protection from Pests and Diseases

In general, bulbs are remarkably free of pests and diseases. Many are poisonous, such as daffodils and hyacinths, and therefore are naturally repellent to damage by rodents. Tulips can present a problem wherever rodents or deer are prolific, since squirrels and mice find the tubers particularly tasty, and the leaves are a favorite food of deer. To discourage rodent damage, sprinkle rodent-repellent flakes or moth balls over the soil where bulbs are planted. To discourage deer from eating the top growth of flowering bulbs, spray the emerging leaves with Repel. This is absorbed by the leaves, making the plant distasteful past the blooming period.

Some bulbs are susceptible to maggot damage and other harmful worms that work their way into the soil. Others, like dahlias, have such succulent foliage growth that they are susceptible to attack by slugs, aphids, thrips, mites, and other chewing insects. Soil pests are extremely difficult to exterminate completely; however, chewing insects are easily controlled by insecticidal sprays that can be purchased from garden centers.

Two good organic insecticides to consider are insecticidal soap and those that combine rotenone and pyrethrum. Rotenone is a natural insecticide made from the roots of a tropical tree; pyrethrum is made from the petals of an African daisy. Together, they offer broad and effective control.

CHAPTER TWO

THE ENCYCLOPEDIA OF ESSENTIAL BULBS

T HE FOLLOWING SECTION DESCRIBES 100 bulbs for spring, summer, or autumn display. Most of them are hardy, but some of them are tender. Many hardy varieties will not survive the winter in frost-free areas, and many tender varieties will not survive the winter in areas where the ground freezes. Often, hardy varieties can be grown in the south by treating them as annuals, while tender varieties can be grown in the north by lifting them in autumn, after frost has killed the tops, and storing the bulbs in a cool, frost-free area.

Each bulb featured here is listed first by its botanical (Latin) name, since this consistently identifies the bulb better than does its common name. While many bulbs have popular common names—'Daffodils' for *Narcissus* species—others do not have such familiar common names or else are widely known by two or more common names—*Lycoris squamigera*, for example, is often called 'Naked Ladies' or 'Magic Lily.'

To find a description for any bulb where you know only the common name, simply refer to the index for a quick cross-reference.

The heights given are mostly mature heights, when the plants start to flower. Often, in good soil or after abundant rainfall, plants may exceed the heights stated here.

BOTANICAL NAME *Acidanthera bicolor*

COMMON NAME Peacock Flower

RANGE Native to South Africa. Hardy zone 6 south.

HEIGHT 2 to 3 feet; erect habit.

CULTURE Easy to grow in any well-drained garden soil in full sun. The brown corms are 1 to 2 inches across. Plant in spring, 2 to 3 inches deep, 3 to 6 inches apart. Summer-flowering.

DESCRIPTION The orchid-like flowers are pure white with handsome purple-brown markings at the petal base. The leaves are long, slender and iris-like. Best grown as an accent in mixed beds and borders. Excellent for cutting. Similar to gladiolus in habit and appearance.

BOTANICAL NAME *Agapanthus africanus*

COMMON NAME African Lily, Lily-of-the-Nile

RANGE Native to South Africa. Hardy zone 8 south.

HEIGHT 3 feet; erect habit.

CULTURE Prefers fertile, moist, sandy soil in sun or partial shade. Plant the rhizomes in the fall, 2 inches deep, 12 to 24 inches apart. Summer-flowering.

DESCRIPTION Large terminal flowers. Clusters can be 10 inches across in shades of blue plus white. Leaves are straplike, forming a thick clump. Best grown in a mass in beds and borders. Popular as a patio or greenhouse pot plant.

RECOMMENDED VARIETIES 'Peter Pan', a dwarf hybrid 2 feet high; also 'Headbourne Hybrids' for increased hardiness.

BOTANICAL NAME *Allium christophii*

COMMON NAME Star-of-Persia

RANGE Native to Turkestan. Hardy zone 4 south to zone 8.

HEIGHT 2 feet; erect habit.

CULTURE Easy to grow in any well-drained garden soil in full sun. Requires warm, dry conditions during its summer rest period. Plant bulbs in fall, 4 inches deep above the bulb, spaced 12 inches apart. Spring-flowering.

DESCRIPTION Purple, starlike flowers form a large umbel up to 8 inches across. Blue-green, fleshy leaves are flat and straplike. Good for massing in mixed beds and borders. Good for cutting and for dried-flower arrangements. Planted in a mass, the flowers produce a billowing, cloudlike effect that is especially dramatic when seen against a background of evergreens.

BOTANICAL NAME *Allium giganteum*

COMMON NAME Giant Allium

RANGE Native to the Himalaya Mountains. Hardy zone 4 south to zone 8.

HEIGHT 4 to 5 feet; erect habit.

CULTURE Prefers fertile, humus-rich loam soil in full sun. Plant bulbs in fall, 6 inches deep above the bulb nose, spaced 12 inches apart. Spring-flowering.

DESCRIPTION Clusters of purple, star-shaped flowers form perfect globes up to 6 inches across on tall, slender stems. The fleshy, blue-green leaves are strap-shaped. Popular planted en masse in mixed beds and borders. Good for cutting. A mass planting of about 8 to 15 bulbs in a mixed bulb and perennial border is a real traffic-stopper.

BOTANICAL NAME *Allium moly*

COMMON NAME Lily Leek

RANGE Native to Southern Europe. Hardy zone 4 south to zone 7.

HEIGHT 12 inches; low-growing, clump-forming habit.

CULTURE Prefers well-drained, fertile, humus-rich loam soil in sun or partial shade. Plant bulbs in fall, 2 inches deep above bulb nose, spaced 6 inches apart. Spring-flowering.

DESCRIPTION Masses of starry yellow flowers form in clusters on slender stems, among onion-like leaves. Popular for edging paths, beds, and borders; also suitable for rock gardens. With its tendency to cluster, this is a good choice for creating a ground cover effect.

BOTANICAL NAME *Allium schoenoprasum*

COMMON NAME Chives

RANGE Native to Europe and Asia. Hardy zone 4 south to zone 8.

HEIGHT 12 inches; spreading, clump-forming habit.

CULTURE Prefers a well-drained, fertile, humus-rich soil in full sun. Plant bulbs in spring or fall, 2 inches deep above the bulb nose, spaced 8 inches apart. Spring-flowering.

DESCRIPTION Clusters of lilac to purple, star-studded flowers form a perfect globe on a slender stem above pungent, hollow, pointed leaves. Popular for rock gardens, herb gardens, pot culture, and massed as an edging for beds and borders. The long, onion-flavored leaves are a favorite flavoring for soups and salads, and the flowers are so abundant that the plants can be grown purely for ornamental effect.

BOTANICAL NAME *Alstroemeria aurantiaca*

COMMON NAME Peruvian Lily

RANGE Native to South America. Hardy zone 7 south.

HEIGHT 2 to 3 feet; erect, clump-forming habit.

CULTURE Prefers a fertile, sandy loam soil in sun or partial shade. Plant tubers 6 inches deep from the tops, 12 inches apart in spring or fall. Summer-flowering.

DESCRIPTION Orange flower clusters have conspicuous orange-red stripes towards the petal centers. Hybrids include a color range of white, pink, red, and purple. Leaves are narrow, arching, and swordlike. Popular for massing in mixed beds and borders. Excellent for cutting. Suitable for growing in containers under glass in the northern United States. Other popular types of Peruvian Lily include *A. pelegrina* (lavender flowers resembling azaleas) and 'Ligtu' hybrids in a rich assortment of bold colors, including red, yellow, and orange.

BOTANICAL NAME *Amaryllis belladonna*

COMMON NAME Naked Ladies, Belladonna Lily

RANGE Native to South Africa. Hardy zone 9.

HEIGHT 2 feet; erect, colony-forming habit.

CULTURE Prefers sandy loam soil in full sun. Plant bulbs in spring, 4 inches deep above bulb nose. Fall-flowering.

DESCRIPTION There is much confusion between the genus *Amaryllis* and *Hippeastrum*, which are often referred to as amaryllis. *A. belladonna* bears a cluster of funnel-shaped, pink flowers on fleshy, slender, leafless stems, similar to *Lycoris squamigera*, also known as Naked Ladies. After the flowers die, green, straplike leaves emerge and thrive until midsummer. Mostly used for naturalizing in open meadows and rock gardens in mild climate areas.

BOTANICAL NAME *Anemone blanda*

COMMON NAME Grecian Windflower

RANGE Native to Asia Minor. Hardy zone 4 south to 8.

HEIGHT 4 inches; low, spreading habit.

CULTURE Prefers a moist, humus-rich loam soil in sun or partial shade. Plant tubers 4 inches deep above the tuber, spaced 2½ inches apart in fall. Early spring-flowering.

DESCRIPTION Purple, rose, and white daisy-like flowers close at dusk and during bad weather. With its dainty, fern-like foliage, they are mostly planted in colonies to produce a mass of bloom over several weeks. Good for naturalizing.

RECOMMENDED VARIETIES 'Rosea' (pink) and 'White Splendor.' Suitable for rock gardens, especially planted in a crescent around a boulder.

BOTANICAL NAME *Anemone coronaria*

COMMON NAME French Anemone, Poppy Anemone

RANGE Native to the Mediterranean. Hardy zone 8 south.

HEIGHT 9 inches; erect habit.

CULTURE Prefers a well-drained, humus-rich sandy or loam soil in sun or partial shade. Plant tubers 4 inches from top of tuber, spaced 3 inches apart in fall. In northern climates, can be grown only under cold frames. Spring-flowering.

DESCRIPTION Poppy-like flowers are red, blue, or white with a conspicuous crown of powdery black anthers at the petal center.

RECOMMENDED VARIETIES 'de Caen' (single-flowered) and 'St. Brigid' (double-flowered). Popular for mass planting in mixed beds and borders, and also as a pot plant. 'Mona Lisa,' a special large-flowered strain, is grown from seed under glass for cutting.

BOTANICAL NAME *Babiana stricta*

COMMON NAME Baboon Flower

RANGE Native to South Africa. Hardy zone 8 south.

HEIGHT 8 inches; clump-forming habit.

CULTURE Easy to grow in any well-drained loam or sandy soil, in full sun. Plant bulbs in fall, 3 inches deep, spaced 3 inches apart. Spring-flowering.

DESCRIPTION Clusters of sweetly scented flowers in blue, rose, and pink are produced freely over several weeks. Foliage is sword-shaped, dark green, and velvety. Exquisite in rock gardens and mixed beds and borders. Protected and mulched during winter, the tender bulbs can be left outdoors up to zone 6.

BOTANICAL NAME *Begonia* x *tuberhybrida*

COMMON NAME Tuberous Begonia

RANGE Native to the Andes. Hardy zone 10.

HEIGHT 18 inches; erect, bushy habit.

CULTURE Prefers moist, humus-rich soil in partial shade. Plant corms in spring after danger of frost, 1 inch deep above crown, spaced 12 inches apart. In areas subject to frost, corms must be lifted in fall and stored in a cool, frost-free area. Summer-flowering.

DESCRIPTION Large, rounded flowers up to 8 inches across, held erect on fleshy stems. Leaves are heart-shaped and toothed. Color range includes red, pink, yellow, orange, and white—some are bicolored. Popular for planting in shady beds and borders, also in window boxes and tubs. Some varieties suitable for hanging baskets. Excellent pot plant for growing under glass.

Right: A beautiful border of tuberous begonias *(Begonia* x *tuberhybrida)* at Butchart Garden, Victoria, British Columbia.

BOTANICAL NAME *Belamcanda chinensis*

COMMON NAME Blackberry-Lily

RANGE Native to China. Hardy zone 5 south.

HEIGHT 3 feet; erect, clump-forming habit.

CULTURE Easy to grow in any well-drained loam soil in full sun. Plant rhizomes 2 inches deep, spaced 6 inches apart in spring or fall. Summer-flowering.

DESCRIPTION Exotic orange flowers are spotted red and cluster at the top of strong, slender stems. Leaves are narrow, arching, and grasslike. After flowers fade, decorative seed pods form, revealing shiny black seeds as the pods dry. Popular for massing in mixed beds and borders. Both the flowers and the dried pods with seeds are good for cutting. A hybrid between *Belamcanda* and *Pardanthopsis*, called 'Candy Lilies,' has an extremely rich color range, including yellow, orange, pink, and white.

BOTANICAL NAME *Bletilla striata*

COMMON NAME Chinese Orchid

RANGE Native to China. Hardy zone 8 south.

HEIGHT 2 feet; upright habit.

CULTURE Outdoors, prefers moist, humus-rich, fertile, loam soil in partial shade. Indoors, grow in a 6-inch pot, using a peat-based potting soil. Plant rhizomes 4 inches deep, 4 to 6 inches apart in the fall. Spring-flowering.

DESCRIPTION The flowers are perfect miniatures of purple or white "Cattleya Orchids." Leaves are dark green, ribbed, broad, and pointed. Popular for woodland wildflower gardens and shady borders in mild climate areas. Easy-to-grow, flowering pot plant for northern states.

BOTANICAL NAME *Caladium* x *hortulanum*

COMMON NAME Rainbow Plant

RANGE Native to South America. Hardy zone 9 south.

HEIGHT 2 to 3 feet; arching, clump-forming habit.

CULTURE Prefers fertile, moist, humus-rich soil in partial shade. Plant tubers, with bumps up, 2 inches deep above the crown, spaced 4 inches apart in fall in frost-free areas; spring elsewhere. Summer-flowering.

DESCRIPTION Heart-shaped, heavily veined leaves, mostly in combinations of white, red, pink, and green, remain decorative all summer. White Jack-in-the-pulpit-like flower spathe is inconspicuous. Popular for massing in beds and borders. Excellent for containers. Plants are tender, must be set outside after danger of spring frost, and lifted for storage indoors before heavy fall frost.

RECOMMENDED VARIETIES 'Candidum' (white with green veins), 'Rosebud' (pink, white, and green), and 'Postman Joyner' (crimson with green edge).

BOTANICAL NAME *Camassia scilloides*

COMMON NAME Wild Hyacinth

RANGE Native to Oregon and British Columbia. Hardy zone 5 south to zone 8.

HEIGHT 12 inches; erect, spirelike habit.

CULTURE Prefers a well-drained, humus-rich soil in full sun. Plant bulbs 4 inches deep above bulb nose, spaced 3 inches apart in fall. Spring-flowering.

DESCRIPTION Blue starlike flowers form a loose flower spike. Grasslike leaves die down soon after flowering. Planted mostly in groups in mixed beds and borders. Good for naturalizing, especially in meadows and rock gardens. *C. esculenta* ('Quamash'), a closely related species is also good for garden display and produces edible bulbs used by Native North Americans as a food staple.

Left: The rainbow plant *(Caladium x hortulanum)* is popular in southern gardens because of its ability to tolerate the heat and periods of low rainfall.

BOTANICAL NAME *Canna* x *generalis*

COMMON NAME Canna

RANGE Hybrids of species native to South America. Hardy zone 8 south.

HEIGHT 4 to 6 feet; erect, towering habit.

CULTURE Prefers moist, humus-rich, well-drained soil in full sun. Plant bulbs 4 inches deep above bulb nose, spaced 12 inches apart after danger of frost in spring. In areas subject to freezing, bulbs must be lifted in fall and stored in a dark, cool, frost-free room. Summer-flowering.

DESCRIPTION Huge, gladiolus-like flowers form terminal flower spikes on strong, erect stems with green or bronze leaves that are tropical in appearance, resembling banana leaves. Color range includes red, pink, orange, yellow, and cream. Popular as an accent in mixed beds and borders, particularly as a background.

RECOMMENDED VARIEITES 'The President,' a large-flowering red.

BOTANICAL NAME *Cardiocrinum giganteum*

COMMON NAME Himalayan Lily

RANGE Native to the Himalayas. Hardy zone 7 south.

HEIGHT 6 to 12 feet; erect, spirelike habit.

CULTURE Prefers moist, well-drained, humus-rich soil loaded with leaf mold in partial shade. Plant bulbs in fall, placing the crown just below soil surface, 2 to 3 feet apart. Early summer-flowering.

DESCRIPTION Gleaming white, trumpet-shaped, lily-like flowers have maroon stripes inside the petals. Borne in clusters, they form a spike on top of a tall, fleshy stem. Large, heart-shaped leaves are glossy dark green, forming rosettes until the flower spike elongates. Mostly grown as a tall background among azaleas and rhododendrons in woodland.

BOTANICAL NAME *Chionodoxa luciliae*

COMMON NAME Glory-of-the-snow

RANGE Native to Asia Minor. Hardy zone 4 south to zone 7.

HEIGHT 4 inches; low, clump-forming habit.

CULTURE Easy to grow in any well-drained garden soil in sun or partial shade. Plant bulbs 4 inches deep above the bulb nose in fall. Early spring-flowering.

DESCRIPTION Dainty blue or pink starlike flowers have white centers, 6 to 12 flowers crowded to a stem. Leaves are smooth and slender. Popular for planting drifts in rock gardens. Also can be naturalized in woodland under deciduous trees.

BOTANICAL NAME *Clivia miniata*

COMMON NAME Kafir-Lily

RANGE Native to South Africa. Hardy zone 9 south.

HEIGHT 2 feet; low-growing, colony-forming habit.

CULTURE Prefers moist, well-drained, fertile, humus-rich loam soil in partial shade. Plant blubs (actually fleshy roots) in fall, 6 inches deep from the base of the roots with the crown just below soil surface, and 12 inches apart or in 12-inch pots. Spring- and early summer-flowering.

DESCRIPTION Trumpet-shaped flowers are clustered to make a dome on top of a thick stalk. Leaves are dark green, straplike, arching, and evergreen. Colors include orange, orange-red, and yellow. Popular in mild climate areas for growing under trees. In northern states mostly grown in pots. Likes to be pot-bound.

BOTANICAL NAME *Colchicum autumnale*

COMMON NAME Autumn-Crocus

RANGE Native to Europe and Africa. Hardy zone 5 south.

HEIGHT 8 inches; low-growing, clump-forming habit.

CULTURE Prefers fertile, moist, well-drained, humus-rich soil in sun or partial shade. Plant corms 3 to 4 inches deep from the crown, spaced 6 to 9 inches apart in summer. Late summer- and early fall-flowering.

DESCRIPTION Plants resemble giant crocus with rose-pink flowers, which appear after the large, straplike leaves have died. Double-flowered forms are available. Popular for edging paths, beds, and borders. Can be naturalized in rock gardens and grassy slopes.

RECOMMENDED VARIETY *C. speciosum*, with flowers that resemble pink water lilies.

BOTANICAL NAME *Colocasia esculenta*

COMMON NAME Elephant's Ear, Giant Taro

RANGE Native to tropical Pacific. Hardy zone 10 only.

HEIGHT 6 to 7 feet; erect, clump-forming habit.

CULTURE Prefers moist, fertile, humus-rich soil in partial shade. Plant corms 3 to 4 inches deep from the nose, spaced at least 4 feet apart after all danger of frost in spring. Corms must be lifted in the fall after frost and stored indoors until the following spring. Summer-flowering.

DESCRIPTION Massive heart-shaped green leaves can grow 5 feet long and 3 feet across. Popular as accents in beds and borders, and in large containers. Especially attractive planted along stream banks and pond margins. Corms are edible, used to make poi, a Polynesian food staple.

BOTANICAL NAME *Convallaria majalis*

COMMON NAME Lily-of-the-valley

RANGE Native to Europe. Hardy zone 3 south to 7.

HEIGHT 6 inches; low, spreading habit.

CULTURE Easy to grow in any well-drained soil in sun or partial shade. Tolerates drought. Plant rhizomes 1 inch deep, 4 inches apart in fall. Spring-flowering.

DESCRIPTION Highly fragrant, white or pink bell-shaped flowers are borne on arching stems, which are produced among the broad, pointed, bright green leaves. Popular as a ground cover to edge paths and borders. Commonly forced in pots to flower indoors in winter. Good for cutting to make dainty flower arrangements.

BOTANICAL NAME *Crinum* x *powellii*

COMMON NAME Summer Amaryllis

RANGE Native to Central and South America. Hardy zone 8 south.

HEIGHT 2 feet; upright habit.

CULTURE Easy to grow in any well-drained loam or sandy soil in full sun. Plant bulbs 6 inches deep from the top of the bulb, spaced 12 inches apart in fall. Summer-flowering.

DESCRIPTION Clusters of large pink or white trumpet-shaped flowers are borne on succulent stems, surrounded by arching, straplike, bright green leaves. Popular for seaside gardens in mild climate areas, where it may naturalize. Makes an attractive accent in mixed beds and borders.

Right: A sunny slope decorated with mostly early-flowering tulip species.

BOTANICAL NAME *Crocosmia* x *crocosmiiflora*

COMMON NAME Montbretia

RANGE Native to South Africa. Hardy zone 6 south.

HEIGHT 3 to 4 feet; erect, clump-forming habit.

CULTURE Prefers a fertile, well-drained, humus-rich soil in sun or partial shade. Plant corms in fall or spring, 3 inches deep, spaced 4 inches apart. Summer-flowering.

DESCRIPTION Orange-red, freesia-like flowers are borne on slender, arching stems. Bright green leaves are swordlike. Popular for massing in mixed beds and borders. Excellent for cutting. Forms thick clumps, which may need dividing after three years.

BOTANICAL NAME *Crocus chrysanthus*

COMMON NAME Snow Crocus

RANGE Native to Greece. Hardy zone 4 south.

HEIGHT 3 inches; low, clump-forming habit.

CULTURE Easy to grow in any well-drained garden soil in full sun. Plant corms 4 inches deep above the corm, spaced $2\frac{1}{2}$ inches apart in fall. Early spring-flowering.

DESCRIPTION Yellow, white, and violet-blue flowers are borne on short stalks above narrow, green, grasslike leaves. Popular for mass planting in rock gardens and as an edging for walks, beds, and borders. Good for naturalizing and pot culture.

RECOMMENDED VARIETIES 'Snow Bunting' (white), 'Blue Pearl,' and 'E.P. Bowles' (yellow).

BOTANICAL NAME *Crocus flavus*

COMMON NAME Yellow Crocus

RANGE Native to Greece and Yugoslavia. Hardy zone 4 south to 8.

HEIGHT 4 inches; low, colony-forming habit.

CULTURE Easy to grow in any well-drained garden soil in full sun. Plant corms 4 inches deep above corm, spaced 2½ inches apart in fall. Early spring-flowering.

DESCRIPTION Golden yellow flowers, clustered several to each corm. Leaves are green, spiky, and upright. This species is often mixed with *C. vernus*, the common crocus, to make a mixture that includes yellow, as well as white and purple. Popular for edging paths, beds, and borders. Suitable for naturalizing in lawns. Good for pot culture.

RECOMMENDED VARIETY 'Yellow Mammoth.'

BOTANICAL NAME *Crocus tomasinianus*

COMMON NAME Snow Crocus

RANGE Native to Dalmatia. Hardy zone 4 south to zone 8.

HEIGHT 3 inches; low, colony-forming habit.

CULTURE Prefers well-drained, humus-rich loam soil in sun or partial shade. Plant corms in fall, 4 inches deep above the corm, spaced 2½ inches. Early spring-flowering.

DESCRIPTION Purple flowers from each bulb are produced in small clusters. Petals with prominent orange-yellow stamens open almost flat on sunny days. Leaves are dark green with a prominent white midrib. Self-seeds to form extensive colonies. Good for rock gardens and woodland. Will grow and bloom through grass.

Left: A bulb border featuring tulips, grape hyacinths *(Muscari armeniaca)*, and tall crown imperials *(Fritillaria imperialis)*.

BOTANICAL NAME *Crocus vernus*

COMMON NAME Common Crocus, Dutch Crocus

RANGE Native to the Pyrenees, Alps, and Carpathian Mountains. Hardy zone 4 south to zone 8.

HEIGHT 4 inches; low, colony-forming habit.

CULTURE Easy to grow in any well-drained garden soil in full sun. Plant corms in fall, 4 inches deep above corm, spaced 2½ inches apart. Early spring-flowering.

DESCRIPTION Purple, white, and bicolor striped flowers clustered several to each corm. Dark green with white midribs, the leaves appear after flowers fade. Popular for edging paths, beds, and borders. Suitable for naturalizing in lawns. Good for pot culture. It is a parent of many large-flowering varieties.

RECOMMENDED VARIETY 'Pickwick' (striped).

BOTANICAL NAME *Cyclamen neopolitanum*

COMMON NAME Hardy Cyclamen

RANGE Native to Greece. Hardy zone 6 south to zone 8.

HEIGHT 6 inches; low-growing, colony-forming habit.

CULTURE Prefers moist, humus-rich loam soil in partial shade. Plant corms in spring, 2 inches deep above crown, spaced 3 inches apart. Fall-flowering.

DESCRIPTION Flowers in pink or white are perfect miniatures of florists' cyclamen. Leaves are ivy-shaped, with silver markings. Popular for naturalizing in shady wildflower gardens and in sink gardens.

RELATED SPECIES *C. purpurascens* and *C. coum*, both spring-flowering.

BOTANICAL NAME *Cyclamen persicum*

COMMON NAME Florists' Cyclamen

RANGE Native to Greece. Hardy zone 9 south.

HEIGHT 6 to 12 inches; low-growing, clump-forming habit.

CULTURE Mostly grown indoors as a pot plant. Prefers moist, humus-rich (peat-based) soil in sun or shade. Plant corms so the crown is just below the soil surface, spaced 3 inches apart. Blooms in early spring from fall-planted bulbs when grown outdoors. Winter-flowering when grown indoors in a cool window or greenhouse.

DESCRIPTION Flowers have swept-back petals that face down and are borne at the top of slender stems. Leaves are decorative, heart-shaped, and sometimes bicolored green and silver. Colors include red, rose-pink, purple, and white. Popular for growing in beds and borders outdoors in frost-free areas. Excellent pot plant.

BOTANICAL NAME *Dahlia pinnata* hybrids

COMMON NAME Dahlia

RANGE Native to Mexico. Hardy zone 9 south.

HEIGHT Up to 6 feet; erect, shrubby habit.

CULTURE Plant tubers in spring after all danger of frost, 6 inches deep from the nose, spaced at least 12 inches apart for dwarf varieties, 2 to 3 feet apart for tall or giant flowering kinds. Tall kinds need strong stakes. Tubers must be lifted after first fall frost and stored indoors until following spring. Summer-flowering.

DESCRIPTION Flowers are highly variable among varieties, including formal decorative types with rounded, double heads and smooth petals to cactus-flowered types with narrow, quill-like petals. Flower size varies from 2-inch pompon type to dinner-plate size, up to 14 inches across. Color range includes white, yellow, orange, purple, pink, red, and bicolors. Stems are fleshy; leaves are bright green and indented. Popular as an accent in mixed beds and borders. Good for cutting if cut ends are scorched.

RECOMMENDED VARIETIES: 'Mary Elizabeth' (cherry red blooms up to 14 inches across) and 'Croydon Ace' (yellow flowers up to 12 inches across).

BOTANICAL NAME *Eranthis hyemalis*

COMMON NAME Winter Aconite

RANGE Native to Europe. Hardy zones 4 to 7.

HEIGHT 2 inches; low, clump-forming habit.

CULTURE Prefers a well-drained, humus-rich soil in sun or partial shade. Especially likes leaf mold. Plant tubers in fall, 4 inches deep above the tuber, spaced 2½ inches apart. Early spring-flowering.

DESCRIPTION Shimmering yellow flowers resembling buttercups appear before the leaves. Leaves are dark green and deeply indented. Popular for planting in woodland where it naturalizes freely from self-seeding. Often blooms during early spring thaws when snow still covers the ground.

BOTANICAL NAME *Eremurus elwesii*

COMMON NAME Foxtail Lily

RANGE Native to Asia. Hardy zone 5 south.

HEIGHT 6 to 10 feet; erect, spirelike habit.

CULTURE Prefers fertile, well-drained loam soil in full sun. Plant the tuberous roots in early fall, splayed out like an octopus with crown covered by 3 inches of soil. Summer-flowering.

DESCRIPTION Fringed white florets form a towering, pointed flower spike, held erect by a strong, slender stem. Leaves are sword-shaped, like a yucca. Popular for tall backgrounds in mixed beds and borders (especially with a tall hedge behind to provide shelter from wind). Other species include yellow and pink flowers.

RECOMMENDED VARIETY 'Shelford Hybrids' a dwarf form 4 to 5 feet in lovely pastel shades.

BOTANICAL NAME *Erythronium* 'Pagoda'

COMMON NAME Dogtooth Violet

RANGE Hybrid of species native to West Coast of North America. Hardy zone 4 south to 9.

HEIGHT 10 inches; erect, colony-forming habit.

CULTURE Prefers a well-drained, humus-rich soil in sun or partial shade. Plant tubers in fall, 4 inches deep above crown, spaced 4 inches apart. Early spring-flowering.

DESCRIPTION Yellow flowers have swept-back petals on a slender stem. Leaves are broad and pointed. Popular for rock gardens and woodland wildflower gardens.

RELATED SPECIES *E.montanum* ('Glacier Lily'),white with orange throat; *E. grandiflorum* ('Avalanche Lily'), yellow with white throat.

BOTANICAL NAME *Eucharis grandiflora*

COMMON NAME Amazon-Lily

RANGE Native to South America. Hardy zone 9 south.

HEIGHT 2 feet; erect habit.

CULTURE Prefers well-drained, moist, humus-rich soil in partial shade or under glass in pots. Plant bulbs in fall, with tops showing through the soil. Spring-flowering outdoors, winter-flowering indoors.

DESCRIPTION Nodding white flowers resemble small-cupped daffodils, opening in an umbel at the top of a slender stem. Leaves are broad, pointed, and glossy dark green. Mostly grown in pots under glass in northern states. In mild climate areas they are grown in shady beds and borders. Excellent for cutting.

Right: The hybrid Lily "Imperial crimson" grows best in a lightly shaded location.

BOTANICAL NAME *Eucomis comosa*

COMMON NAME Pineapple Lily

RANGE Native to South Africa. Hardy zone 7 south.

HEIGHT 2 feet; erect, colony-forming habit.

CULTURE Prefers moist, fertile, sandy soil in full sun. Plant bulbs in spring, 3 inches deep from nose of bulb, spaced 12 inches. Summer-flowering.

DESCRIPTION Star-shaped, lime green florets are densely clustered at the top of a strong, slender flower spike with a top-knot of spiky leaves resembling a pineapple. Leaves are dark green and straplike. In mild climate areas they are good for mixed beds and borders. Popular in northern states for growing in pots under glass.

BOTANICAL NAME *Freesia* x *hybrida*

COMMON NAME Freesia

RANGE Native to South Africa. Hardy zone 9 south.

HEIGHT 1 1/2 to 2 feet; arching habit.

CULTURE Prefers to be grown in 6-inch pots under glass, using a peat-based potting soil. Plant corms in fall with the point just below the soil surface, 6 to a pot. Store in a cool, dark place for 4 weeks, then move to a sunny location for flowering (10 to 12 weeks later). Lift and store corms through summer months. Spring-flowering.

DESCRIPTION Arching flower spikes are crowded with fragrant crocus-like florets in white, yellow, orange, pink, red, and purple. Leaves are narrow, long, and sword-shaped.

BOTANICAL NAME *Fritillaria imperialis*

COMMON NAME Crown Imperial

RANGE Native to Iran. Hardy zone 4 south to zone 6.

HEIGHT 2 feet; erect habit.

CULTURE Prefers well-drained, fertile, humus-rich soil in sun or partial shade. Plant bulbs in fall, 6 inches deep above the bulb nose, spaced 12 inches apart. The bulbs should be planted on their sides to keep water from collecting in the hollow on top of the bulb and rotting it. Spring-flowering.

DESCRIPTION Orange and yellow bell-shaped flowers hang from thick, succulent stalks. A tuft of green, spiky leaves crown the flower head. Longer pointed leaves crowd the stem. If cut or bruised the leaves produce a smell that pervades the air with a skunklike odor. Popular for mixed beds and borders; also planted at the edge of woodland.

BOTANICAL NAME *Fritillaria meleagris*

COMMON NAME Checkered Lily

RANGE Native to Europe. Hardy zone 4 south to 8.

HEIGHT 8 inches; erect, clump-forming habit.

CULTURE Easy to grow in any well-drained garden soil in sun or partial shade. Plant bulbs in fall, 4 inches deep above the bulb nose, $2\frac{1}{2}$ inches apart. Spring-flowering.

DESCRIPTION Nodding, bell-shaped, white or purple flowers with a dark, checkered pattern on the petals. Leaves are thin, inconspicuous, and grasslike. Popular for rock gardens, wildflower meadows, and woodland gardens.

BOTANICAL NAME *Galanthus elwesii*

COMMON NAME Snowdrop

RANGE Native to Europe and West Asia. Hardy zone 4 south to zone 7.

HEIGHT 4 to 6 inches; low-growing, clump-forming habit.

CULTURE Prefers a well-drained, fertile, humus-rich soil, particularly one with leaf mold. Plant bulbs in fall, 4 inches deep above the bulb nose, spaced 2½ inches apart. Early spring-flowering.

DESCRIPTION Nodding white tear-drop-shaped flowers are held above the slender green foliage on erect stems. There is a double form, 'Flore Pleno.' Good for edging paths, beds, and borders, and for naturalizing in woodland. Bulbs increase readily by division and also self-seed.

BOTANICAL NAME *Gladiolus* x *hortulanus*

COMMON NAME Gladiolus

RANGE Native to South Africa. Hardy zone 6 south to zone 8.

HEIGHT 3 to 4 feet; erect, spirelike habit.

CULTURE Prefers fertile, well-drained loam soil in full sun. Plant corms 2 to 3 inches deep from the crown, spaced 12 inches apart in spring after ground has thawed. Plants may need staking. North of zone 6, gladiolus corms can be lifted in fall and stored indoors to survive winter. Summer-flowering.

DESCRIPTION Ruffled, open-throated florets are studded along tall, slender stems, forming beautiful flower spikes. Leaves are sword-shaped and ribbed, like irises. Color range includes yellow, white, orange, pink, red, purple, and bicolors. Popular for mixed beds and borders as a background. Excellent for cutting.

RECOMMENDED VARIETIES 'St. Patrick's' (green flowers) and 'Red Spire' (dark red).

BOTANICAL NAME *Gloriosa rothschildiana*

COMMON NAME Rothchild Gloriosa-Lily

RANGE Native to Africa. Hardy zone 10.

HEIGHT 3 to 8 feet; vining, climbing habit.

CULTURE Prefers a fertile, well-drained loam soil in full sun. Plant tubers in 6-inch pots covered with 2 inches of soil in a heated greenhouse or sun room. After flowering, withhold water to induce dormancy, lift bulbs and store among dry woodshavings for 3 months, then repot and water. Several flowering cycles can be had each year. Needs staking. Can be planted outdoors in northern climates after danger of frost for summer-flowering.

DESCRIPTION Crimson flowers have ruffled, yellow petal edges and prominent yellow stamens projecting forward. Leaves are dark green and spear-shaped. Popular for growing under glass in pots.

BOTANICAL NAME *Haemanthus katharinae*

COMMON NAME Katharine Blood-Lily

RANGE Native to South Africa. Hardy zone 10.

HEIGHT 12 inches; erect habit.

CULTURE Best grown in 6-inch pots using a peat-based, well-drained potting soil in full sun. Plant bulbs in fall, one to a pot, with the bulb nose projecting through the soil surface. When foliage withers in summer, withhold water to induce dormancy and revive its growth cycle in early fall. Winter- and early spring-flowering.

DESCRIPTION Globular, bristlelike, bright red flower heads up to 9 inches across are borne on top of a strong, slender stem. White and pink kinds also available. Spectacular pot plant for growing under glass.

BOTANICAL NAME *Hemerocallis fulva*

COMMON NAME Tawny Daylily

RANGE Native to China. Hardy zone 4 south.

HEIGHT 3 to 4 feet; erect, clump-forming habit.

CULTURE Easy to grow in any well-drained garden soil. Plant tubers so they angle down with the tip 1 inch below the soil surface. Summer-flowering.

DESCRIPTION Orange flowers are trumpet-shaped. Leaves are long, slender, and grasslike. Hybrids have expanded color range to include cream, yellow, red, purple, maroon, and bicolors. Popular for massing in beds and borders, also for naturalizing.

RECOMMENDED VARIETIES 'Hypericon' (yellow) and 'Red Siren' (dark red).

BOTANICAL NAME *Hippeastrum hybrida*

COMMON NAME Amaryllis

RANGE Hybrids of species native to South America. Hardy zone 9 south.

CULTURE Prefers a fertile, well-drained, humus-rich garden soil or peat-based potting soil when grown in pots. Plant bulbs in fall, so that the nose is slightly above soil surface, spaced 12 inches apart. Winter-flowering indoors, spring-flowering outdoors in mild climates.

DESCRIPTION Huge trumpet-shaped flowers, up to 10 inches across, bloom 4 to a stem atop fleshy, hollow stalks. Leaves are broad, arching and straplike. Color range includes red, white, orange, pink, and bicolors. Mostly grown in 6-inch pots in northern states. Popular in beds and borders in southern gardens.

BOTANICAL NAME *Hyacinthoides hispanica*

COMMON NAME Spanish Bluebell

RANGE Native to Europe. Hardy zone 6 south.

HEIGHT 15 inches; erect habit.

CULTURE Prefers fertile, moist, humus-rich soil in partial shade. Plant bulbs in fall, 3 inches deep above the bulb nose, spaced 6 inches apart. Spring-flowering.

DESCRIPTION Nodding, blue, bell-shaped flowers are highly fragrant and clustered at the top of arching stems. Leaves are green and sword-shaped. Popular for woodland gardens, where they will naturalize. Excellent for cutting. Similar in appearance to English Bluebells *(H. non-scriptus)*, but generally a little more showy and more reliable for North America.

BOTANICAL NAME *Hyacinthus orientalis*

COMMON NAME Dutch Hyacinth

RANGE Native to Mediterranean countries. Hardy zone 4 south to zone 8.

HEIGHT 8 to 10 inches; erect habit.

CULTURE Prefers fertile, humus-rich loam soil in full sun. Plant bulbs in fall, 6 inches deep from the bulb nose, spaced 6 inches apart. Spring-flowering.

DESCRIPTION Highly fragrant, star-shaped florets are closely set around a thick, fleshy stem, producing an erect flower column above several green, straplike leaves. Color range includes red, blue, pink, yellow, white, and purple. Good for massing in beds and borders. Popular for pot culture. Prechilled bulbs are offered by many bulb dealers for growing in special hyacinth vases, filled only with water.

RECOMMENDED VARIETIES 'Delft Blue,' 'Haarlem' (yellow), 'Lady Derby' (rose-pink), and 'Jan Bos' (red).

Right: Spanish Bluebells
(Hyacinthoides hispanica)
naturalized beside a stream.

BOTANICAL NAME *Hymenocallis narcissiflora*

COMMON NAME Peruvian Daffodil, Ismene

RANGE Native to Peru. Hardy zone 8 south.

HEIGHT 2 feet; upright habit.

CULTURE Prefers a fertile, humus-rich, well-drained soil in sun or partial shade. North of their hardiness range, plant bulbs in spring after the ground thaws, 3 to 4 inches deep above the crown, spaced 12 inches apart. Summer-flowering.

DESCRIPTION Fragrant white flowers have long, reflexed petals and a daffodil-like trumpet at the petal center. The flowers are borne on top of slender stems among arching, straplike leaves. Popular for mixed beds and borders, also as a flowering pot plant. Naturalizes freely and creates colonies in frost-free areas.

BOTANICAL NAME *Incarvillea delvayii*

COMMON NAME Hardy Gloxinia

RANGE Native to China. Hardy zone 6 south.

HEIGHT 12 inches; low, rosette-forming habit.

CULTURE Prefers well-drained, fertile, humus-rich acid soil in sun or partial shade. Plant tubers in fall with tips angled down just below the soil surface, spaced 8 inches apart. Spring-flowering.

DESCRIPTION Lovely trumpet-shaped, pink or rosy red blooms have purple and yellow throats and are clustered at the top of slender stems. Leaves are glossy, dark green, heavily veined, and indented. Popular for rock gardens.

BOTANICAL NAME *Iris cristata*

COMMON NAME Crested Iris

RANGE Native to North America. Hardy zone 5 south to zone 8.

HEIGHT 6 inches; low, spreading habit.

CULTURE Prefers well-drained, humus-rich loam soil in sun or shade. Plant rhizomes in fall, with tips just below soil surface, spaced 6 inches apart. Spring-flowering.

DESCRIPTION Blue or white flowers carpet the ground among broad, spear-shaped, green leaves. Popular for rock gardens and edging woodland paths. Naturalizes freely.

BOTANICAL NAME *Iris danfordiae*

COMMON NAME Danford Iris

RANGE Native to Asia Minor. Hardy zone 4 south to 8.

HEIGHT 4 to 6 inches; low, erect, colony-forming habit.

CULTURE Prefers well-drained, humus-rich loam soil in full sun. Plant bulbs in fall, 4 inches deep above the bulb nose, spaced 2 to 5 inches apart. Early spring-flowering.

DESCRIPTION Typical iris flowers are golden yellow, striking through the soil even before the last snowfall. Narrow, pointed leaves appear after flowering. Mostly planted in small drifts in rock gardens.

Left: Clumps of bearded iris *(Iris germanica* hybrids) in the Iris Garden at the Ladew Topiary Gardens, near Monkton, Maryland.

BOTANICAL NAME *Iris* x *germanica*

COMMON NAME Bearded Iris

RANGE Hybrids of species native to Europe. Hardy zone 4 south.

HEIGHT 3 feet; erect, clump-forming habit.

CULTURE Easy to grow in any well-drained loam soil in full sun. Plant rhizomes in fall, with the crown level to the soil surface, spaced 6 to 12 inches apart. Early summer-flowering.

DESCRIPTION The showiest of all irises, bearded iris' fragrant flowers bloom in a spectacular range of colors, including white, pink, red, blue, purple, orange, and maroon. Many are bicolored, with a contrasting yellow cluster of powdery stamens known as the "beard." Three curving upright petals—called "standards"—and three wide drooping petals called "falls"—make up the distinctive large flower heads, which are held aloft on thick stems. Leaves are bright green, sword-shaped, and decorative even when the plants are not in bloom. Excellent for massing to make a "rainbow" bed or border. Popular for cutting.

BOTANICAL NAME *Iris hollandica*

COMMON NAME Dutch Iris

RANGE Developed from species native to Spain and North Africa. Hardy zone 8 south to zone 9.

HEIGHT 2 to 3 feet; erect habit.

CULTURE Prefers moist, fertile, humus-rich soil in sun or partial shade. Plant bulbs in fall, 3 inches deep, 4 inches apart. Spring-flowering.

DESCRIPTION Mostly blue, yellow, and white flowers, which are held erect on slender stems with spiky green leaves. They are graceful plants and extremely popular for cutting. Mostly massed in beds and borders.

BOTANICAL NAME *Iris kaempferi*

COMMON NAME Japanese Iris

RANGE Native to Japan. Hardy zone 5 south.

HEIGHT 2 to 3 feet; erect habit.

CULTURE Prefers moist, fertile, humus-rich loam soil in full sun. Plant rhizomes in fall, the tips just below the soil surface and spaced 12 inches apart. Tolerates boggy conditions. Early summer-flowering.

DESCRIPTION Mostly blue, purple, and white flowers with flattened heads (compared to other irises), on stiff stems among handsome, green, sword-shaped leaves. Popular for massing in beds and borders. Especially beautiful when planted along stream beds and pond margins.

BOTANICAL NAME *Iris reticulata*

COMMON NAME Dwarf Blue Iris

RANGE Native to the Caucasus Mountains. Hardy zone 4 south to 8.

HEIGHT 6 inches; low, colony-forming habit.

CULTURE Prefers well-drained, fertile, humus-rich soil in full sun. Plant bulbs in fall, 4 inches deep above the bulb nose, spaced 2½ inches apart. Spring-flowering.

DESCRIPTION Mostly purple and blue flowers, typically iris in shape. Sometimes sold in a mixture with *I. danfordiae* to introduce yellow into the color range. Leaves are narrow, green, and spiky. Popular planted in small drifts for rock gardens, also for forcing in containers.

BOTANICAL NAME *Ixia maculata*

COMMON NAME Corn-Lily

RANGE Native to South Africa. Hardy zone 7 south to zone 9.

HEIGHT 15 inches; erect, spreading habit.

CULTURE Prefers a fertile, humus-rich loam soil in full sun. Plant corms in fall, 4 inches deep above the crown, spaced 2½ inches apart. Spring-flowering.

DESCRIPTION Starlike flowers on tall, wiry stems with swordlike leaves. Color range includes cream, yellow, purple, and rose. Popular for mixed beds and borders and for rock gardens. Hardy in mild climate areas.

BOTANICAL NAME *Leucojum vernum*

COMMON NAME Spring Snowflake

RANGE Native to Europe. Hardy zone 4 south.

HEIGHT 9 inches; low-growing, clump-forming habit.

CULTURE Prefers a moist, well-drained, humus-rich soil in partial shade. Plant bulbs in fall, 3 inches deep above bulb nose, spaced 3 inches apart. Spring-flowering.

DESCRIPTION Dainty, pendulous, white flowers cluster along short, arching stems with narrow, pointed leaves. Popular for naturalizing in woodland and shade gardens. Often flowers before the last snowfalls of spring.

RELATED SPECIES *L. aestivum* ('Summer Snowflake') growing to 2 feet with larger flowers, especially in the variety 'Graveyte Giant.'

BOTANICAL NAME *Lilium auratum*

COMMON NAME Oriental Lily

RANGE Native to Japan. Hardy zone 5 south.

HEIGHT 4 to 6 feet; erect habit.

CULTURE Prefers fertile, well-drained, humus-rich soil in partial shade. Plant bulbs in fall, 4 inches deep above the crown, spaced 2 feet apart. Summer-flowering.

DESCRIPTION Magnificent white flowers with flared, reflexed petals measure up to 10 inches across, have yellow stripes down the center of each petal and exotic red spots. Prominent red stamens protrude far from the petals. Leaves are green and lance-shaped. Popular accent to mixed beds and borders. Exquisite for cutting. Hybrids such as the superlative 'Imperial' strain have been developed from *L. auratum*, including red and pink flowering kinds.

BOTANICAL NAME *Lilium candidum*

COMMON NAME Madonna Lily, Bermuda Lily

RANGE Place of origin unknown though probably Asia. Hardy zone 4 south.

HEIGHT 38 inches; erect, spirelike habit.

CULTURE Prefers a well-drained, humus-rich, sandy soil in full sun. Plant bulbs in fall, 4 inches deep above bulb nose, spaced 12 inches apart. Summer-flowering.

DESCRIPTION Large, white, trumpet-shaped blooms are borne at the top of a thick, fleshy stem with green, straplike leaves. Though considered hardy, *L. candidum* can be difficult to establish unless drainage is perfect. Popular for mixed beds and borders and for mass plantings. Good for cutting. Can be forced in pots.

Right: Easter Lilies *(Lilium longiflorum)* massed in an island bed.

BOTANICAL NAME *Lilium hybrida 'asiatic'*

COMMON NAME Asiatic Hybrid Lilies

RANGE Developed from species native to Asia. Hardy zone 4 south to 7.

HEIGHT 2 to 5 feet; erect habit.

CULTURE Prefers moist, well-drained, humus-rich soil in partial shade. Plant bulbs in fall, 4 inches deep above the crown, spaced 12 inches apart. Summer-flowering.

DESCRIPTION The 'Mid-Century' strain of asiatic hybrid lilies is especially beautiful. The upward facing flowers measure up to 6 inches across in a wide assortment of colors, including red, yellow, white, orange, pink, lavender, and mahogany. Strong, slender stems have lancelike leaves. Popular for naturalizing in woodland gardens. Also planted as accents in mixed beds and borders. Superb for cutting.

RECOMMENDED VARIETY 'Enchantment,' which possesses a lovely range of colors.

BOTANICAL NAME *Lilium longiflorum*

COMMON NAME White Trumpet Lily

RANGE Native to Japan. Hardy zone 8 south.

HEIGHT 3 to 4 feet; erect habit.

CULTURE Prefers well-drained, humus-rich soil in full sun. Plant bulbs in fall, 4 inches deep above the crown, spaced 12 inches apart. Summer-flowering.

DESCRIPTION Fragrant and elegant, pure white, trumpet-shaped flowers are clustered at the top of slender stems. Leaves are lancelike. Popular for massing in mixed beds and borders. Exquisite for cutting. The variety *'eximium'* is especially well known as the Easter Lily, which is forced under glass in pots in time for Easter.

BOTANICAL NAME *Lilium superbum*

COMMON NAME Turkscap Lily

RANGE Native to North America. Hardy zone 5 south.

HEIGHT 5 to 6 feet; erect habit.

CULTURE Prefers moist, fertile, humus-rich loam soil in sun or partial shade. Plant bulbs in fall, 3 inches deep above the crown, spaced 12 inches apart. May need staking. Summer-flowering.

DESCRIPTION Orange-red flowers with recurved petals have yellow throats and exotic red spots. Its nodding flowers are clustered on top of a slender stem. Leaves are dark green and lancelike. Popular for massing in mixed beds and borders. Good for cutting.

BOTANICAL NAME *Lycoris radiata*

COMMON NAME Red Spider Lily

RANGE Native to Japan. Hardy zone 7 south.

HEIGHT 12 to 18 inches; erect habit.

CULTURE Easy to grow in any well-drained garden soil in sun or partial shade. Plant bulbs in spring, 3 inches deep, spaced 6 inches apart. Fall-flowering.

DESCRIPTION Rich red florets have narrow, reflexed petals and prominent, arching anthers, which give the flower clusters a spidery appearance. These flowers are borne on top of slender, naked stems. Leaves are narrow, pointed, and straplike. Popular for edging paths, beds, and borders. Also grown in containers. Excellent for cutting.

BOTANICAL NAME *Lycoris squamigera*

COMMON NAME Naked Ladies

RANGE Native to Japan. Hardy zone 5 south.

HEIGHT 2 feet; erect, colony-forming habit.

CULTURE Prefers well-drained, fertile, sandy soil in full sun. Plant bulbs in spring or fall, 4 inches deep from bulb nose, spaced 6 inches apart. Summer-flowering.

DESCRIPTION Pink, trumpet-shaped flowers appear at the top of a thick, fleshy stem after the straplike leaves have died. Popular as an accent in mixed beds and borders, and for naturalizing in drifts. Closely related to amaryllis.

BOTANICAL NAME *Muscari armeniacum*

COMMON NAME Grape Hyacinth

RANGE Native to Asia Minor. Hardy zone 4 south to zone 8.

HEIGHT 5 inches; low, clump-forming habit.

CULTURE Easy to grow in any well-drained garden soil in sun or partial shade. Plant bulbs in fall, 4 inches deep above the bulb nose, spaced 3 inches apart. Spring-flowering.

DESCRIPTION Tiny, bell-shaped, blue flowers are clustered on top of slender stems above narrow, pointed leaves. Readily increases by division of the bulbs and by self-seeding. Popular for edging paths, beds, and borders, also for naturalizing in rock gardens.

BOTANICAL NAME *Narcissus* x *hybrida* 'Double-flowered'

COMMON NAME Double-Flowered Daffodil

RANGE Developed from species native to Europe. Hardy zone 3 south to 9.

HEIGHT 20 inches; erect, clump-forming habit.

CULTURE Easy to grow in any fertile, well-drained loam soil in sun or partial shade. Plant bulbs in fall, 4 inches deep above the bulb nose, spaced 6 inches apart. Spring-flowering.

DESCRIPTION Fragrant flowers are mostly yellow or white and fully double, with a contrasting yellow or orange bicolor effect towards the petal center. Good as accents in mixed beds and borders. Sensational cut flower; also good for forcing in pots.

BOTANICAL NAME *Narcissus* x *hybrida* 'Trumpet-flowered'

COMMON NAME Trumpet Daffodil

RANGE Developed from species native to Europe. Hardy zone 3 south to 9.

HEIGHT 20 inches; erect, clump-forming habit.

CULTURE Easy to grow in any well-drained, fertile, garden loam in sun or partial shade. Plant bulbs in fall, 4 inches deep above the bulb nose, spaced 6 inches apart. Spring-flowering.

DESCRIPTION Mostly golden yellow or white, plus bicolored flowers with a prominent trumpet. The most popular of all daffodils for massing in beds and borders or naturalizing in meadows, lawns, and along stream banks and pond margins. Wonderful cut flower. Good for forcing in pots.

BOTANICAL NAME *Narcissus minimum*

COMMON NAME Miniature Daffodil

RANGE Native to Europe. Hardy zone 4 south to zone 8.

HEIGHT 6 inches; clump-forming habit.

CULTURE Easy to grow in any well-drained loam soil in sun or partial shade. Plant bulbs in fall, 4 inches deep from the top of the bulb, spaced 4 inches apart. Early spring-flowering.

DESCRIPTION Clusters of dainty, golden yellow, trumpet blooms are borne above long, pointed leaves. They are perfect miniatures of their larger cousins, the golden trumpet-flowered daffodil, excellent for naturalizing, and also popular for growing in pots. Other popular small-flowered species include *N. bulbocodium* ('Hoop Petticoat Daffodils') and *N. cyclamineus*, having reflexed, outer petals.

BOTANICAL NAME *Narcissus poeticus*

COMMON NAME Poet's Daffodil, Pheasant's Eye

RANGE Native to Greece. Hardy zone 3 south to 8.

HEIGHT 20 inches; erect, clump-forming habit.

CULTURE Easy to grow in any fertile, well-drained loam soil in sun or partial shade. Plant bulbs in fall, 4 inches deep above the bulb nose, spaced 6 inches apart. Spring-flowering.

DESCRIPTION White flowers have small, white or yellow frilly cup with orange rim. Leaves are narrow and pointed. Popular for naturalizing in deciduous woodland and along stream banks and pond margins. Superb for cutting.

BOTANICAL NAME *Narcissus triandrus*

COMMON NAME Daffodil, Angels-Tears

RANGE Native to Spain. Hardy zone 4 to 8.

HEIGHT 12 inches; erect, clump-forming habit.

CULTURE Easy to grow in any well-drained garden soil in sun or partial shade. Plant bulbs in fall, 4 inches deep above bulb nose, and 4 inches apart. To grow in zone 9 south, precool bulbs 8 to 10 weeks at 40° to 45°F prior to planting in early December. Early spring-flowering.

DESCRIPTION White or yellow flowers clustered on slender stems. Leaves are long and narrow. Popular for mixed beds and borders. Excellent for cutting. Can be naturalized if fed a high-phosphorus fertilizer in spring before bulbs bloom and again in fall.

RECOMMENDED VARIETY 'Thalia,' a gleaming white.

BOTANICAL NAME *Nerine bowdenii*

COMMON NAME Nerine

RANGE Native to South Africa. Hardy zone 9 south.

HEIGHT 12 inches; erect habit.

CULTURE Easy to grow in any fertile, well-drained soil or sandy potting soil in sun or partial shade. Outdoors, plant bulbs in spring, leaving the bulb tips above the soil surface, spaced 3 to 4 inches apart. Indoors, plant in fall under glass. Summer-flowering outdoors, winter-flowering indoors.

DESCRIPTION Funnel-shaped flowers form terminal umbels on slender stalks above straplike green leaves. Colors include white, pink, and red. Popular for pot culture in the North and rock gardens in mild climate areas.

Right: Mass plantings of grape hyacinths *(Muscari armeniacum)* at Keukenhoff Bulb Garden (Holland).

BOTANICAL NAME *Ornithogalum thyrsoides*

COMMON NAME Chincherinchee

RANGE Native to South Africa. Hardy 8 south.

HEIGHT 12 to 18 inches; erect, colony-forming habit.

CULTURE Prefers sandy loam soil in full sun. Plant bulbs in fall, 2 inches deep above the bulb nose, and spaced 2 inches apart. Spring-flowering.

DESCRIPTION White, starlike florets have dark centers and form a pointed cluster on top of a slender stem. Leaves are narrow, pointed, and grass-like. Naturalizes easily in mild climates. Popular for mixed beds and borders. Good for containers. Excellent for cutting.

BOTANICAL NAME *Ornithogalum umbellatum*

COMMON NAME Star of Bethlehem

RANGE Native to Europe; naturalized throughout North America. Hardy zone 4 south.

HEIGHT 6 inches; low, clump-forming habit.

CULTURE Easy to grow in any well-drained garden soil in sun or partial shade. Plant bulbs in fall, 4 inches deep above the bulb nose, and spaced 2½ inches apart. Spring-flowering.

DESCRIPTION Starlike flowers are white; leaves are narrow and pointed. Usually forms dense clumps by division of bulbs and self-seeding. Popular for edging paths and naturalizing in rock gardens.

BOTANICAL NAME *Oxalis pes-caprae*

COMMON NAME Bermuda Buttercup

RANGE Native to South Africa. Hardy zone 9 south.

HEIGHT 12 inches; low-growing, spreading habit.

CULTURE Easy to grow in any well-drained garden soil in full sun. Outdoors, plant bulbs in fall, 2 inches deep above the bulb nose, and spaced 3 inches apart. Outdoors, early spring-flowering in mild climate areas; indoor, winter-flowering under glass.

DESCRIPTION Bright yellow, buttercup-like flowers are borne on slender stems above shamrock-like plants. Suitable for pots and hanging baskets. Naturalizes freely in open sunny locations.

BOTANICAL NAME *Pleione formosa*

COMMON NAME Fairy Orchid

RANGE Native to Formosa and China. Hardy zone 9 south.

HEIGHT 6 inches; low, colony-forming habit.

CULTURE Outdoors, prefers moist, humus-rich, fertile loam soil in partial shade. Indoors, best grown in 4-inch pots, using a peat-based potting soil. Plant corms in fall, 2 inches deep above the crown, and spaced 4 inches apart. Corms remain dormant from October through February. Spring-flowering.

DESCRIPTION Lovely pink or white orchid flowers have speckled throats and an exotic fringed lip. They are borne on slender stems above arching, pointed leaves. Good for growing massed in beds under deciduous shrubs that provide bright light in spring and cool shade in summer. Popular for growing in pots.

Left: The Fosteriana tulip 'Orange Emperor' massed in a sunny bed at Lentenboden Bulb Garden, near New Hope, Pennsylvania.

BOTANICAL NAME *Polianthus* x *tuberosa*

COMMON NAME Tuberose

RANGE Native to Mexico. Hardy zone 7 south.

HEIGHT 2 to 3 feet; erect, spirelike habit.

CULTURE Prefers moist, fertile, humus-rich loam soil in full sun. Plant rhizomes in spring, 2 inches deep above the crown and spaced at least 6 inches apart. Lift rhizomes after flowering and store indoors even in areas where they are considered hardy. Late summer-flowering.

DESCRIPTION Highly fragrant, gardenia-like white flowers are clustered in a spike on top of a slender stem. Dark green leaves are broad and long, like gladiolus. Popular for mixed beds and borders. Exceptional for cutting.

BOTANICAL NAME *Puschkinia scilloides*

COMMON NAME Striped Squill

RANGE Native of Caucasus Mountains and Asia Minor. Hardy zone 4 south to 8.

HEIGHT 6 inches; upright, clump-forming habit.

CULTURE Easy to grow in any well-drained garden soil in full sun. Plant bulbs in fall, 4 inches deep above the bulb nose, and spaced $2^{1}/_{2}$ inches apart. Spring-flowering.

DESCRIPTION Bluish white flowers are star-shaped and clustered at the top of a slender stem. Green leaves are straplike. Popular for naturalizing in rock gardens. Increases by division of bulbs and self-seeding.

BOTANICAL NAME *Ranunculus asiaticus*

COMMON NAME Persian Buttercup

RANGE Native to Greece, Turkey, and Persia. Hardy zone 8 south.

HEIGHT 12 to 18 inches; erect habit.

CULTURE Outdoors in mild climates, plant tubers in fall in any well-drained, humus-rich, garden soil in full sun. Cover with 3 inches of soil, spacing tubers 6 inches apart. Indoors, grow in a peat-based potting soil, with sand added for good drainage, 4 tubers to each 5-inch pot. After flowering, lift bulbs and store for 3 to 4 months before repotting. Outdoors, early spring-flowering; indoors, winter-flowering.

DESCRIPTION Lovely double flowers have petals that look like crèpe paper, in a rich color range that includes yellow, white, orange, pink, and red. The flowers are held erect on long stems. Leaves are deeply indented and fern-like. Popular in mild climates for mixed beds and borders. Good for cutting and containers.

BOTANICAL NAME *Scilla peruviana*

COMMON NAME Peruvian Squill

RANGE Native to South America. Hardy zone 8 south.

HEIGHT 12 inches; clump-forming habit.

CULTURE Easy to grow in any well-drained loam or sandy soil in sun or partial shade. Plant bulbs in fall, 4 inches deep from the top of the bulb, and spaced 4 inches apart. Spring-flowering.

DESCRIPTION Umbels of star-shaped blue flowers are borne on slender stems among bright green, straplike leaves. Mostly grown as a pot plant under glass. Resembles a miniature Blue Agapanthus.

BOTANICAL NAME *Scilla siberica*

COMMON NAME Siberian Squill

RANGE Native to the Caucasus Mountains. Hardy zone 4 south.

HEIGHT 5 inches; low growing, erect, clump-forming habit.

CULTURE Easy to grow in any well-drained garden soil in sun or partial shade. Plant bulbs in fall, 4 inches deep above the bulb nose, and spaced 3 inches apart. Early spring-flowering.

DESCRIPTION Each bulb bears several stems of nodding, bell-shaped blue flowers above straplike leaves. Popular for forming drifts in rock gardens and naturalizing in woodland to form a dense, blue carpet. Increases by bulb division and self-seeding. Often blooms during a thaw while snow is still on the ground.

RECOMMENDED VARIETY 'Spring Beauty,' a sterile selection with extra-large flowers.

BOTANICAL NAME *Sinningia speciosa*

COMMON NAME Gloxinia

RANGE Native to South America. Hardy only indoors.

HEIGHT 12 inches; compact, rosette-forming habit.

CULTURE Best grown indoors as a flowering pot plant. Plant in spring, one tuber to a 6-inch pot, using a peat-based potting soil in partial shade. Plant tubers 1 inch deep above the crown. Keep soil moist at all times. After flowering, the plants may go dormant. Water sparingly until renewed growth begins. Summer-flowering.

DESCRIPTION Magnificent trumpet-shaped flowers can be single or double in mostly white, red, pink, purple, blue, and bicolors with conspicuous speckles in the throat. Leaves are spear-shaped, heavily veined, and velvety in texture. Excellent for growing under lights.

RECOMMENDED VARIETIES 'Emperor Frederick' (red flowers, bordered with white), 'Princess Elizabeth' (rich purple with white throat).

BOTANICAL NAME *Sparaxis tricolor*

COMMON NAME Harlequin Flower

RANGE Native to South Africa. Hardy zone 6 south.

HEIGHT 8 to 10 inches; erect, clump-forming habit.

CULTURE Prefers a well-drained, fertile sandy soil in full sun. Plant corms in fall, 4 inches deep above the crown, and spaced 2½ inches apart. Needs a sheltered, south-facing exposure. Spring-flowering.

DESCRIPTION Six-petaled, starlike flowers are mostly bicolored and tricolored in white, yellow, red, and purple, with handsome dark brown zoning at the petal center. Popular for mixed beds, borders, and containers. Good for cutting.

BOTANICAL NAME *Sprekelia formosissima*

COMMON NAME Jacobean-Lily

RANGE Native to Mexico. Hardy zone 9 south.

HEIGHT 12 inches; erect habit.

CULTURE Easy to grow in any well-drained garden or potting soil. Plant bulbs in fall, with the neck protruding above the soil, and 4 inches apart. Planted in fall to bloom during winter or early spring. Spring-flowering outdoors; winter-flowering under glass.

DESCRIPTION Orchid-like, red flower is borne on a slender stem above a cluster of grasslike green leaves. Popular for growing in rock gardens in mild climates, but mostly grown as a pot plant under glass.

Right: Lily-flowered tulips planted in pots decorate a fountain area at Longue Vue Gardens, in New Orleans, Louisiana.

BOTANICAL NAME *Sternbergia lutea*

COMMON NAME Fall crocus

RANGE Native to Asia Minor. Hardy zone 7 south.

HEIGHT 6 inches; low-growing, clump-forming habit.

CULTURE Prefers fertile, humus-rich loam soil in full sun. Plant bulbs in summer, 4 inches deep from the bulb nose, and spaced 3 to 4 inches apart. Fall- and winter-flowering.

DESCRIPTION Crocus-like yellow flowers are borne on slender stems among grasslike leaves. Foliage persists through winter, and withers away as plants go dormant in spring. Popular for edging paths, beds, and borders. Also good for naturalizing on sunny slopes.

BOTANICAL NAME *Tigridia pavonia*

COMMON NAME Tiger-Flowers, Shell-Flowers

RANGE Native to Mexico. Hardy zone 7 south.

HEIGHT 2 feet; erect habit.

CULTURE Easy to grow in any fertile, well-drained garden soil in full sun. Plant bulbs in spring after danger of frost, 4 inches deep from the bulb nose, and spaced 6 inches apart. Summer-flowering.

DESCRIPTION Exotic, three-petaled flowers are iridescent with handsome red freckles at the petal centers. The leaves are sword-shaped and resemble iris leaves. Color range includes yellow, red, pink, orange, purple, and bicolors. Popular for mixed beds and borders, also pond margins and stream banks. Good for cutting, but the flowers last only a day.

BOTANICAL NAME *Triteleia uniflora*

COMMON NAME Star flower

RANGE Native to Argentina. Hardy zone 6 south to 9.

HEIGHT 5 inches; low, colony-forming habit.

CULTURE Easy to grow in any well-drained garden soil in sun or partial shade. Plant bulbs in fall, 4 inches deep from the bulb nose, and spaced 2½ inches apart. Spring-flowering.

DESCRIPTION Six-petaled, light blue, star-shaped, lightly fragrant flowers. Leaves are narrow, grasslike, and emit an onion odor when bruised. Popular for rock gardens. In warm, sunny, sheltered locations clumps can spread rapidly from bulb division and self-seeding.

BOTANICAL NAME *Tulbaghia violacea*

COMMON NAME Society Garlic

RANGE Native to South Africa. Hardy zone 9 south.

HEIGHT 2 feet; erect, clump-forming habit.

CULTURE Easy to grow in any well-drained garden soil. Plant corms in fall, with crowns just below soil surface in sun or partial shade, spaced 12 inches apart. Summer-flowering.

DESCRIPTION Pink, star-shaped flowers are clustered at the top of a slender stem. Evergreen leaves are narrow, pointed, onion-like, and emit an onion odor when bruised. Popular for creating an evergreen ground cover in mild climate areas. Also effective in mixed beds and borders.

Left: Several varieties of yellow tulips create an attractive naturalistic garden with blue phlox *(Phlox divaricata)* at Afton Villa Gardens, St. Francisville, Louisiana.

BOTANICAL NAME *Tulipa clusiana*

COMMON NAME Candlestick Tulip, Peppermint Stick

RANGE Native to Iran. Hardy zone 4 south to 8.

HEIGHT 12 inches; upright habit.

CULTURE Prefers fertile, humus-rich loam soil in partial shade. Plant bulbs in fall, 2 inches deep above the bulb nose, spaced 6 inches apart. Early spring-flowering.

DESCRIPTION White, urn-shaped flowers have rose-pink undersides and sharply pointed petals. Leaves are long, narrow, and pointed. Popular for massing in rock gardens and mixed borders. Naturalizes freely.

BOTANICAL NAME *Tulipa dasystemon, Tulipa tarda*

COMMON NAME Tulip species

RANGE Native to Asia. Hardy zone 4 south to 8.

HEIGHT 6 inches; low-growing, colony-forming habit.

CULTURE Easy to grow in any well-drained garden soil in full sun. Plant bulbs in fall, 2 inches deep above the bulb nose and 6 inches apart. Early spring-flowering.

DESCRIPTION Bright yellow, star-shaped flowers open out flat on sunny days. Shimmering petals and narrow pointed leaves. Popular for rock gardens and edging mixed borders. Naturalizes freely.

BOTANICAL NAME *Tulipa fosteriana*

COMMON NAME Foster Tulip

RANGE Native to Turkestan. Hardy zone 4 south to 8.

HEIGHT 18 inches; erect habit.

CULTURE Prefers fertile, humus-rich, well-drained loam soil in full sun. Plant bulbs in fall, 6 inches deep above the bulb nose, and 6 inches apart. To grow in zone 9 south, precool bulbs 8 to 10 weeks at 40° to 45°F prior to planting in late November. Early spring-flowering.

DESCRIPTION Shimmering red flowers open out flat in full sun, display a black zone near the petal center, and remain closed on cloudy days. Hybrid varieties expand the color range to yellow, orange, red, and pink. Popular for massing in beds and borders, also good for rock gardens. Plants will naturalize by bulb division if fed with a high-phosphorus fertilizer in spring before flowering and again in fall.

RECOMMENDED VARIETIES 'Red Emperor' and 'Princeps,' both scarlet-flowered.

BOTANICAL NAME *Tulipa greigii*

COMMON NAME Peacock Tulip

RANGE Native to Turkistan. Hardy zone 4 south to 8.

HEIGHT 6 to 9 inches; erect habit.

CULTURE Prefers well-drained, humus-rich, fertile loam soil in full sun. Plant bulbs in fall, 3 inches deep above bulb nose, and spaced 4 inches apart. Early spring-flowering.

DESCRIPTION Flowers are iridescent, mostly opening out flat with pointed petals in sunlight. Leaves are distinctive among tulips—mostly striped green and purple, broad, wavy, pointed, and rosette-forming. Color range includes yellow, red, white, and bicolors. Popular for rock gardens, and for mixed beds and borders.

BOTANICAL NAME *Tulipa* x *hybrida* 'Darwin'

COMMON NAME Darwin Hybrid Tulips

RANGE Hybrids of species native to Asia Minor. Hardy zone 4 south to 9.

HEIGHT 2 feet; erect habit.

CULTURE Prefers well-drained, fertile, humus-rich loam soil in full sun. Plant bulbs in fall, 4 inches deep above bulb nose, and spaced 6 inches apart. Early spring-flowering.

DESCRIPTION Huge, urn-shaped, iridescent blooms are the largest among the tulips—the result of crossing regular Darwin tulips and *Fosteriana* tulips. Color range includes white, yellow, red, orange, pink, and bicolors. Leaves are broad and pointed. The most popular of all tulips for bedding. Though not as long-lasting as regular Darwin tulips, Cottage and Triumph Tulips—which they resemble—are unequaled for sheer brilliance.

BOTANICAL NAME *Tulipa* x *hybrida* 'Lily-Flowered'

COMMON NAME Lily-Flowered Tulip

RANGE Hybrids of species mostly native to Asia. Hardy zone 4 south.

HEIGHT 3 feet; erect habit.

CULTURE Prefers well-drained, fertile, humus-rich loam soil in full sun. Plant bulbs in fall, 4 inches deep above bulb nose, and spaced 8 inches apart. Spring-flowering.

DESCRIPTION Urn-shaped flowers have elegantly pointed petals in white, yellow, pink, red, orange, and purple. Leaves are broad and pointed. Popular as an accent planted in beds and borders.

RECOMMENDED VARIETIES 'Queen of Sheba' (orange-red with yellow petal tips) and 'White Triumphator' (a magnificent pure white).

BOTANICAL NAME *Tulipa* x *hybrida* 'Parrot'

COMMON NAME Parrot-Flowered Tulip

RANGE Hybrids of species native to Asia. Hardy zone 4 to 9.

HEIGHT 2 feet; erect habit.

CULTURE Prefers well-drained, fertile, humus-rich loam soil in full sun. Plant bulbs in fall, 4 inches deep above bulb nose, and spaced 8 inches apart. Spring-flowering.

DESCRIPTION Huge flowers have laciniated petals in yellow, pink, red, white, purple, and bicolors. Leaves are broad and pointed. Mostly massed in groups as an accent in beds and borders. Good for cutting.

BOTANICAL NAME *Tulipa* x *hybrida* 'Peony-flowered'

COMMON NAME Peony-Flowered Tulip

RANGE Hybrids of species mostly native to Asia. Hardy zone 4 south.

CULTURE Prefers well-drained, fertile, humus-rich loam soil in full sun. Plant bulbs in fall, 4 inches deep above bulb nose, and spaced 8 inches apart. Late spring-flowering.

DESCRIPTION Large, fully, double, peony-like flowers are borne facing up among broad, pointed leaves. Color range includes white, yellow, red, pink, orange, purple, and bicolors. Popular for massing in beds and borders.

RECOMMENDED VARIETIES 'Mount Tacoma' (white), 'Angelique' (pink). They are similar to—but with larger flowers that bloom later—Early Double Tulips, which bloom up to 4 weeks earlier in the season.

Right: Just fifteen bulbs of the lily-flowered tulip 'Fellowship' can make a stunning display.

BOTANICAL NAME *Tulipa kaufmanniana*

COMMON NAME Water-Lily Tulip

RANGE Native to Turkestan. Hardy zone 4 south to 8.

HEIGHT 9 inches; low-growing, colony-forming habit.

CULTURE Easy to grow in any well-drained, fertile loam soil in full sun. Plant bulbs in fall, 4 inches deep above the bulb nose, and spaced 4 inches apart. Early spring-flowering.

DESCRIPTION Exceptionally beautiful flowers resembling water lilies. Color range includes white, yellow, red, and a few bicolors with black zoning. Petals remain closed on cloudy days, but open out flat in full sun. Popular for rock gardens and massing in beds and borders. Naturalizes by division of bulbs if fed with high-phosphorus fertilizer in spring before plants bloom and again in fall.

RECOMMENDED VARIETY 'Stresa' (yellow and red).

BOTANICAL NAME *Tulipa praestans*

COMMON NAME Leather-Bulb Tulip

RANGE Native to Bukhara (Russia). Hardy zone 4 south.

HEIGHT 12 inches; low-growing habit.

CULTURE Easy to grow in any fertile, well-drained loam soil in full sun. Plant bulbs in fall, 3 inches deep above the bulb nose, and spaced 6 inches apart. Spring-flowering.

DESCRIPTION Red flowers with pointed petals are borne in clusters of up to four and open at one time among broad, pointed, lancelike leaves. An eye-catching accent for low beds and rock gardens.

RECOMMENDED VARIETY 'Fusilier.'

BOTANICAL NAME *Veltheimia viridifolia*

COMMON NAME Cape Lily

RANGE Native to South Africa. Hardy zone 9 south.

HEIGHT 2 to 3 feet; erect habit.

CULTURE Easy to grow in any fertile, well-drained garden soil or potting soil in full sun. Plant bulbs in mid-summer or early fall, so tops protrude through soil. Space them 6 inches apart. Winter-flowering under glass; spring-flowering outdoors in mild climates.

DESCRIPTION Tubular yellow or pink flowers are clustered on top of a long, slender stem, resembling a 'Red-hot-poker' plant. Leaves are attractively scalloped, forming a rosette. Good as an accent massed in beds and borders. Popular for containers and for growing under glass in northern states. Excellent for cutting.

BOTANICAL NAME *Watsonia pyramidata*

COMMON NAME Bugle Flower

RANGE Native to South Africa. Hardy zone 8 south.

HEIGHT Up to 5 feet; erect habit.

CULTURE Prefers well-drained, fertile, sandy loam soil in full sun. Plant corms in fall, 4 inches deep above the crown, and spaced 6 inches apart. Summer-flowering.

DESCRIPTION Rosy red tubular florets form a flower spike on strong slender stems. Leaves are sword-shaped. Popular in mild climates for massing in mixed beds and borders. Good for cutting. Hybridization has expanded the color range to include white, pink, orange-red, and lavender.

Left: The fringed tulip 'Fancy Frills' lights up a spring flower border.

BOTANICAL NAME *Zantedeschia aethiopica*

COMMON NAME Calla Lily

RANGE Native to Africa. Hardy zone 8 south.

HEIGHT 3 feet; erect, clump-forming habit.

CULTURE Prefers moist, fertile, humus-rich soil in sun or partial shade. Tolerates boggy conditions. Plant rhizomes in summer or fall, 4 inches deep above bulb nose, and spaced at least 12 inches apart. Late spring- and early-summer-flowering.

DESCRIPTION Pristine, fragrant, white flower spathes have powdery yellow pistils protruding from the petal center, which grows from thick, long stems. Leaves are green, wavy, and spear-shaped. Good for planting beside streams and pond margins in mild climates. Naturalizes freely in swampy soil. Popular for growing in 6-inch pots or tubs under glass in northern states. Hybridization has expanded the color range to include yellow, orange, pink, red, and maroon. Variety 'Green Goddess' has an unusual green tip.

BOTANICAL NAME *Zephyranthes atamasco*

COMMON NAME Atamasco Lily, Zephyr Lily

RANGE Native to southern United States. Hardy zone 7 south.

HEIGHT 12 inches; erect, colony-forming habit.

CULTURE Easy to grow in any fertile, well-drained garden soil in sun or partial shade. Plant bulbs in fall, 2 inches deep from bulb nose, and spaced 2 inches apart. Spring-flowering.

DESCRIPTION White, trumpetlike flowers are sometimes tinted pink, and are borne erect on slender stems above narrow, pointed, grasslike leaves. Popular in southern United States for naturalizing in lawns and along stream banks and pond margins. Suitable for pots under glass in northern states.

Left: An informal planting of Triumph tulips brighten a sunny slope.

CHAPTER THREE

GARDEN PLANS

ISLAND BED OF SUMMER-FLOWERING BULBS

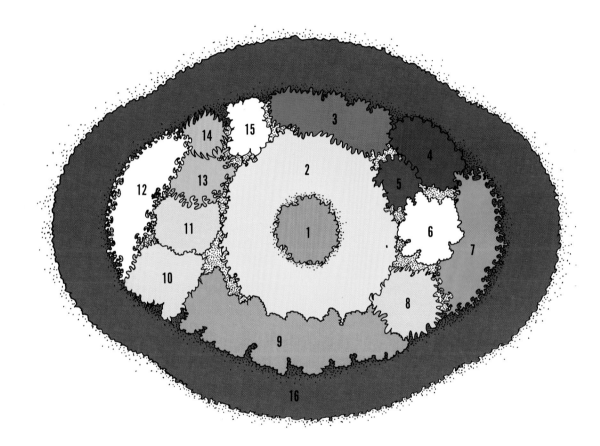

1—Elephant ear, *Colocasia esculenta* (green leaves)
2—Dahlia, *Dahlia pinnata* (mixed colors)
3—Montbretia, *Crocosmia crocosmiiflora* (orange-red)
4—Iris, Bearded iris (blue)
5—Lily, Red spider (red)
6—Lily, White trumpet (white)
7—Lily, African lily, Lily-of-the-Nile (blue)
8—Gladiola, *Gladiolus africanus* (pink)

9—Daylily, *Hemerocallis* (orange)
10—Tiger-flower, *Tigridia pavonia* (mixed colors)
11—Nerine, *Nerine bowdenii* (pink)
12—Lily, Calla (white)
13—Amaryllis, *Crinum* x *powellii* (pink)
14—Lily, Pineapple (lime green)
15—Peacock flower, *Acidanthera bicolor* (white)
16—Rainbow plant, *Caladium* x *hortulanum* (mixed colors)

A. M. Georgens

These tulip borders in a woodland garden feature the Darwin hybrid tulip, 'Beauty of Apeldoorn,' at the entrance to a driveway in Atlanta, Georgia.

INFORMAL BULB BORDER

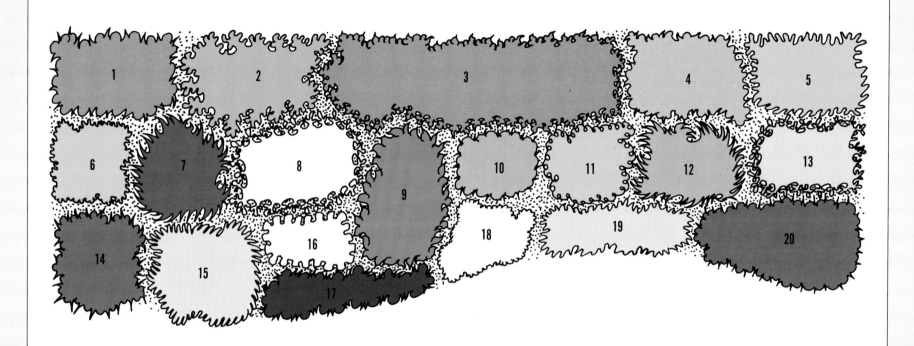

1. Tulip, Single Early, General de Wet (orange)
2. Triumph Tulip, Garden Party (rose pink on white)
3. Crown Imperial 'Aurora' (orange)
4. Triumph Tulip, Apricot Beauty (soft apricot pink)
5. Tulip, Single Early Keizerschoon (yellow and scarlet)
6. Daffodil, Birma (yellow, orange cup)
7. Tulip, Double Early "Stockholm" (scarlet)
8. Daffodil, Ice Follies (white and cream trumpet)
9. Hyacinth, Bismark (porcelain blue)
10. Tulip, Double Early "Peachblossom" (rose pink and white)

11. Daffodil, Golden Harvest (deep yellow)
12. Hyacinth, Princess Margaret (rose pink)
13. Tulip, Double Early (yellow)
14. Tulip, *Fosteriana* 'Printemps' (red)
15. Tulip, Parrot Texas Flame (yellow and red)
16. Hyacinth, *L'Innocence* (white)
17. Grape Hyacinth, *Tete a Tete* (blue)
18. Daffodil, Roulette (white with huge yellow and orange crown)
19. Tulip, Tarda (yellow)
20. Tulip, *Fosteriana* 'Red Emperor'

A. M. Georgens

This rainbow tulip border features mostly different colors of Darwin hybrid tulips.

FORMAL BULB GARDEN

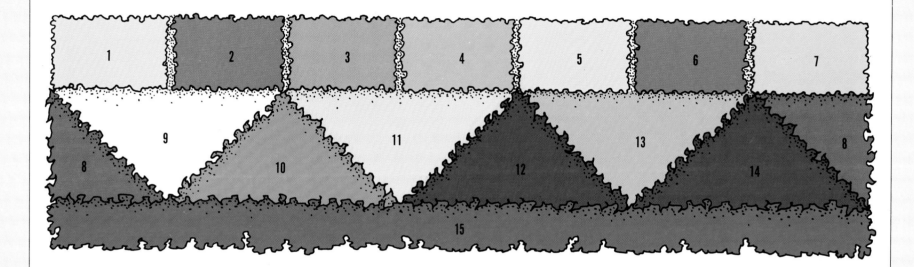

1—Tulip, Darwin Hybrid, Golden Springtime (yellow)
2—Tulip, Darwin Hybrid, General Eisenhower (red)
3—Tulip, Darwin Hybrid, Orange Sun (orange)
4—Tulip, Darwin Hybrid, Big Chief (rose, flushed pink)
5—Tulip, Darwin Hybrid, Beauty of Apeldoorn (yellow and carmine)
6—Tulip, Darwin Hybrid, Volcano (red)
7—Tulip, Darwin Hybrid, Elizabeth Arden (pink)
8—Hyacinth, Jan Bos (deep carmine rose)

9—Hyacinth, *L'Innocence* (pure white)
10—Hyacinth, Bismark (porcelain blue)
11—Hyacinth, City of Haarlem (soft yellow)
12—Hyacinth, Ostara (deep blue)
13—Hyacinth, Lady Derby (pale pink)
14—Hyacinth, Delft's Blue (sapphire blue)
15—Hyacinth, *Muscari armeniacum* (purple)

This small-space bulb garden features borders of tulips, daffodils, and grape hyacinths surrounding a lawn.

WINTER-FLOWERING BULB GARDEN

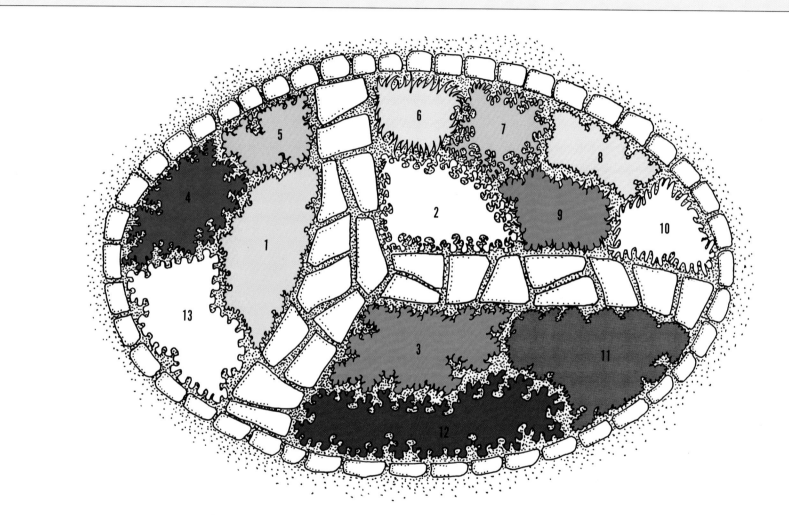

1—Aconite, *Eranthis hyemalis* (yellow)
2—Snowdrop, *Galanthus nivalis* (white)
3—Iris, Early dwarf (blue)
4—Crocus, Snow (purple)
5—Tulip, *Daysystemon* (yellow)

6—Tulip, *Kaufmanniana* (yellow and white bi-color)
7—Narcissus, February Gold (golden yellow)
8—Iris, Dwarf Yellow (yellow)

9—Sibirica Squill, *Scilla siberica* (blue)
10—Windflower, *Anemone blanda* (white)
11—Tulip, *Fosteriana* 'Printemps' (red)
12—Glory of the Snow, *Chionodoxa lucilae* (blue)
13—Leucojum vernum (white)

White snowdrops and yellow aconites naturalized under deciduous trees, are the earliest of spring-flowering bulbs.

ISLAND BED OF FALL-FLOWERING BULBS

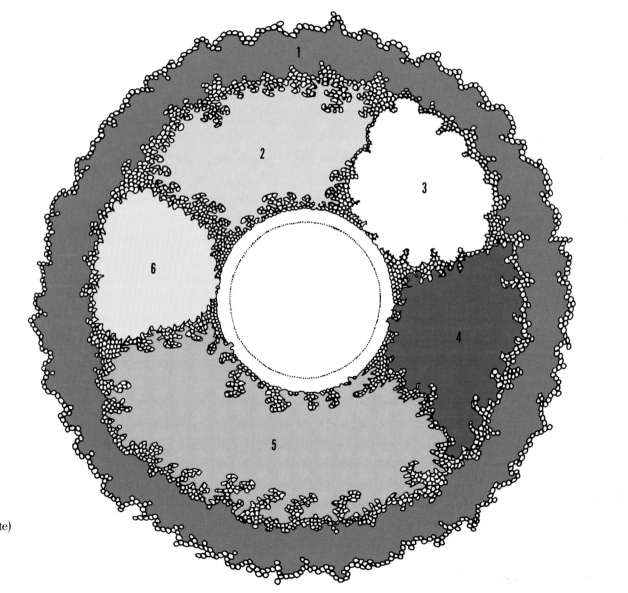

1—Lily, Red Spider (red)
2—Lily, Belladonna (pink)
3—Tuberose, *Polyanthes tuberosa* (white)
4—Colchicum, Hybrids (purple)
5—Crocus, Autumn (pink)
6—Sternbergia, Fall (yellow)

A. M. Georgens

Lily-flowered tulips and Phlox divaricata make good companions in this New Orleans garden.

FORMAL PARTERRE GARDEN OF SPRING-FLOWERING BULBS

1—Tulip, Darwin Hybrid Oxford (red)
2—Daffodil, Stadium, (white with yellow cup)
3—Crown Imperial, *Fritillaria imperialis* (orange)
4—Hyacinth, Delft Blue (blue)
5—Daffodil, Pink Glory (pink)
6—Darwin hybrid tulip, Golden Springtime (gold)
7—Hyacinth, Lady Derby (pink)
8—Crown Imperial, *Fritillaria imperialis* (orange)
9—Daffodil, Birma (yellow with red cup)
10—Hyacinth, *L'Innocence* (white)
11—Lily-flowered tulip, Queen of Sheba (white)
12—Hyacinth, *Tête à Tête* (purple)
13—Tulip, Tarda (yellow)
14—Daffodil, Ice Follies (white with yellow cup)
15—Hyacinth, City of Haarlem (yellow)
16—Lily-flowered tulip, Mariette (pink)
17—Tulip, Red Emperor (red)

After flowering, spaces can be planted with summer-flowering annuals.

A. M. Georgens

The tulip 'Printemps' is thriving in light shade under this crabapple tree.

WATER GARDEN FEATURING SPRING AND SUMMER BULBS

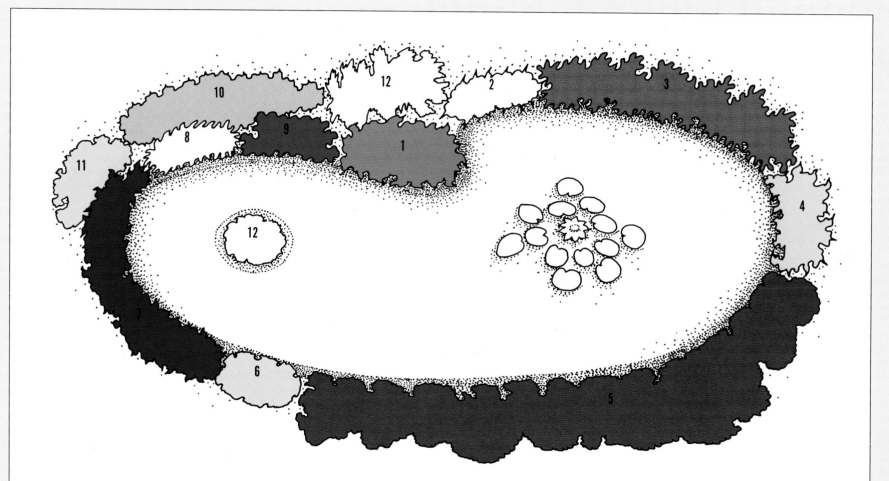

1—Elephant ear, *Colocasia esculenta* (green leaves)
2—Narcissus, Actaea (white, red cup)
3—Canna, *Canna generalis* (red)
4—Iris, Flag Iris (yellow)

5—Rainbow plant, *Caladium* x *hortulanum* (mixed colors)
6—Narcissus, Sempre Avanti, (yellow, gold cup)
7—Iris, Sibirian Iris (blue)
8—Tulip, White Triumphator (white)

9—Iris, Japanese Iris (purple)
10—Tulip, Peony-flowered (mixed colors)
11—Narcissus, Unsurpassable (yellow)
12—Lily, Calla (white)

A. M. Georgens

Left: Sunny slope at Lentenboden bulb garden near New Hope, Pennsylvania, planted with early flowering tulips and hyacinths, beneath the flower-laden branches of a crab apple tree.

FREE-FORM BED OF SPRING AND SUMMER-FLOWERING BULBS

1—Aconite, *Eranthis hyemalis* (yellow)
2—Crocus, *Crocus tomasinianus* (purple)
3—Snowdrop, *Galanthus elwesii* (white)
4—Iris, Dwarf Blue (blue)
5—Narcissus, February Gold (golden yellow)
6—Crocus, Common Crocus, Dutch Crocus (purple)
7—Crown Imperial, *Fritillaria imperialis* (orange)
8—Tulip, Red Emperor (red)
9—Tulip, *Tulipa tarda* (yellow)
10—Tulipa, Double-Fringed Beauty (red and
    yellow bi-color)
11—Hyacinth, *Hyacinthus hispanica* (blue)
12—Crocus, Yellow Crocus (yellow)

13—Wildflower, *Anemone blanda* (white)
14—Lily leek, *Allium moly* (yellow)
15—Crown Imperial, *Fritillaria imperialis* (orange)
16—Tulip, Queen of Sheba (red and yellow bi-color)
17—Striped Squill, *Puschkinia scilloides* (white)
18—Hyacinth, Wild (blue)
19—Narcissus, Roulette (yellow, orange cup)
20—Tulip, Queen of Sheba (red and yellow bi-color)
21—Narcissus, King Alfred (yellow)
22—Hyacinth, Lady Derby (pink)
23—Tulip, Darwin Hybrid Oxford (red)
24—Tulip, Darwin Hybrid Golden Springtime
25—Narcissus, Sempre Avanti (yellow, gold cup)

26—Grape Hyacinth, *Muscari armeniacum* (blue)
27—Tulip, Triumph 'Purissima' (white)
28—Narcissus, Mount Hood (white)
29—Tulip, Parrot 'Karel Doorman' (red)
30—Iris, Wedgewood (blue)
31—Hyacinth, Bismark (dark blue)
32—Tulip, Texas Flame (yellow and red)
33—Narcissus, Red Devon (red)
34—Tulip, Darwin Hybrid Big Chief (red)
35—Spring snowflake, *Leucojum aestivum* (white)
36—Hyacinth, *L'Innocence* (white)

A. M. Georgens

A rock garden featuring crown imperials, Greigii tulips, and daffodils.

CUTTING GARDEN FOR SPRING AND SUMMER BULBS

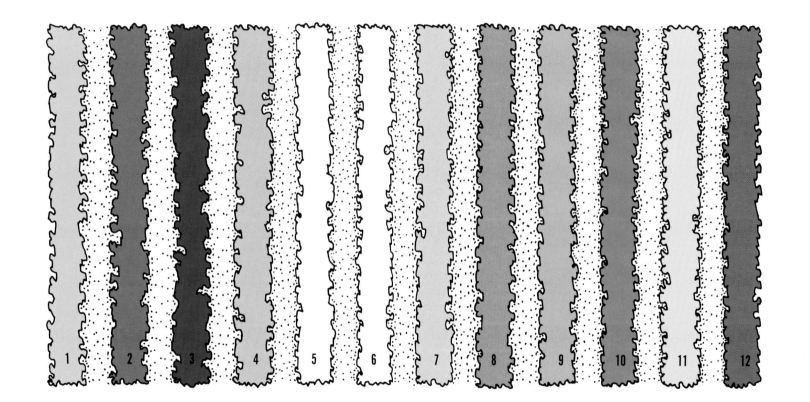

1—Daffodil, Trumpet (mixed colors)
2—Tulip, Darwin Hybrid (mixed colors)
3—Iris, Bearded Iris (mixed colors)
4—Gladiola, Gladiolus (mixed colors)

5—Peacock flower, *Acidanthera* (white)
6—Tuberose, *Polyanthes tuberosa* (white)
7—Dahlia, Hybrids (mixed colors)
8—Lily, Mid-century (mixed colors)

9—Nerine, *Nerine bowdenii* (pink)
10—*Agapanthus africanus* (blue)
11—*Tigridia pavonia* (yellow)
12—*Crocosmia crocosmiiflora* (orange-red)

A. M. Georgens

A border of daffodils brighten a formal bulb garden at the Keukenhoff estate, Holland. This variety is called 'Flower Record.'

ROCK GARDEN FOR SPRING-FLOWERING BULBS

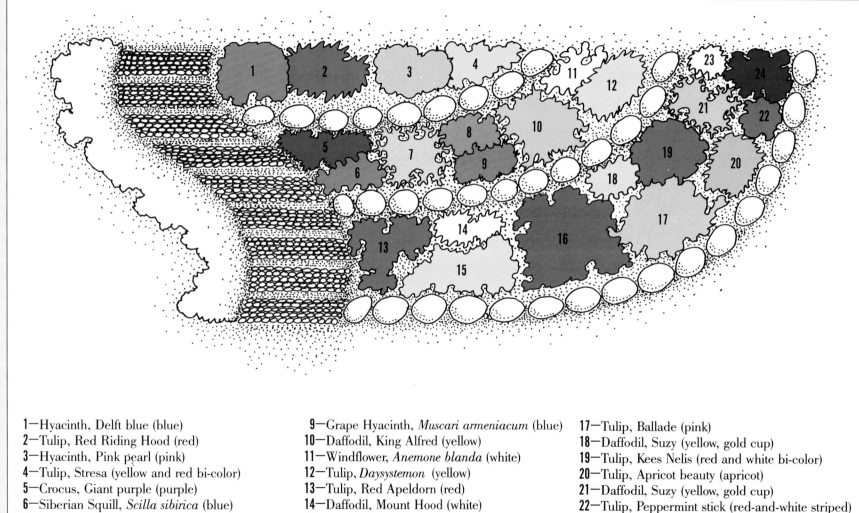

1—Hyacinth, Delft blue (blue)
2—Tulip, Red Riding Hood (red)
3—Hyacinth, Pink pearl (pink)
4—Tulip, Stresa (yellow and red bi-color)
5—Crocus, Giant purple (purple)
6—Siberian Squill, *Scilla sibirica* (blue)
7—Tulip, Gold coin (golden yellow)
8—Crown Imperial, *Fritillaria imperialis* (orange)

9—Grape Hyacinth, *Muscari armeniacum* (blue)
10—Daffodil, King Alfred (yellow)
11—Windflower, *Anemone blanda* (white)
12—Tulip, *Daysystemon* (yellow)
13—Tulip, Red Apeldorn (red)
14—Daffodil, Mount Hood (white)
15—Aconite, *Eranthis hyemalis* (yellow)
16—Tulip, Red Emperor (red)

17—Tulip, Ballade (pink)
18—Daffodil, Suzy (yellow, gold cup)
19—Tulip, Kees Nelis (red and white bi-color)
20—Tulip, Apricot beauty (apricot)
21—Daffodil, Suzy (yellow, gold cup)
22—Tulip, Peppermint stick (red-and-white striped)
23—Snowdrop, *Galanthus nivalis* (white)
24—Dwarf blue iris, *Iris reticulata* (blue)

A. M. Georgens

Crown imperials highlight an informal bulb garden in a woodland setting.

CHAPTER FOUR

PLANT SELECTION GUIDE

Following is a quick reference guide to selecting bulbs for different situations. It is not absolute and the absence of a plant from a particular list does not mean it cannot be used for that specific purpose. For complete information on plant uses, see the encyclopedia section.
*marginally hardy

HARDY

*Acidanthera	Fritillaria
Allium	Galanthus
Anemone blanda	*Gladiolus
Belamcanda	Hemerocallis
Camassia	Hyacinthoides
Chionodoxa	Hyacinthus
Colchicum	Hymenocallis
Convallaria	Incarvillea
*Crocosmia	Iris
Crocus	Leucojum
Cyclamen	Lilium
Eranthis	Muscari
Erythronium	Narcissus
Ornithogalum	Sternbergia
Puschkinia	Tritelia
Scilla	Tulipa

TENDER

Agapanthus	Haemanthus
Alstroemeria	Hippeastrum
Amaryllis	Ixia
Anemone coronaria	Lycoris
Babiana	Nerine
Begonia	Oxalis
Bletilla	Polianthes
Caladium	Pleione
Canna	Ranunculus
Cardiocrinum	Sinningia
Clivia miniata	Sparaxis
Colocussia	Sprekelia
Crinum	Tigridia
Dahlia	Tulbaghia
Eremurus	Veltheimia
Eucharis	Watsonia
Eucomis	Zantedeschia
Gloriosa	Zephyranthes

FALL COLOR

*tender to frost

*Caladium	*Dahlia
*Canna	*Haemanthus
Colchicum	*Gladiolus
*Colocasia	*Lycoris
Crocus sativus	*Polianthes
Cyclamen	Sternbergia

ORNAMENTAL FOLIAGE

*Begonia	Hemerocallis
*Caladium	Iris
*Colocasia	*Zantedeschia
Cyclamen	

SUMMER FLOWER

*Acidanthera	*Gladiolus
*Agapanthus	Hemerocallis
*Alstroemeria	Iris
*Begonia	Lilium
Belamcanda	Nerine
*Canna	Polyanthes
Crocosmia	*Sinningia
*Dahlia	*Tigridia
*Eremurus	*Tulbaghia
*Eucomis	Watsonia

SPRING FLOWER

*Amaryllis
Anemone blanda
*Anemone coronaria
*Bletilla
Camassia
*Cardiocrinum
Chionodoxa
*Clivia
Convallaria
*Crinum
Crocus
Cyclamen
Eranthis
*Eucharis
*Erythronium
Fritillaria
Galanthus
*Gloriosa

Hyacinthoides
*Ixia
Leucojum
Muscari
Narcissus
Ornithogalum
Oxalis
*Pleione
Puschkinia
Ranunculus
Scilla
*Sparaxis
*Sprekelia
*Tritelia
Tulipa
*Veltheimia
*Zantedeschia
*Zephyranthes

SHADE TOLERANT

*Amaryllis
*Begonia
*Bletilla
*Caladium
Chionodoxa
Cyclamen
Eranthis
*Eucharis
Erythronium

Fritillaria
Galanthus
Hyacinthoides
Lilium
Narcissus
Scilla
*Sinningia
*Zantedeschia
*Zephyranthes

MOISTURE TOLERANT

*Canna
*Colocasia
Iris kaempferi
Iris pseudacorus
*Zantedeschia

Opposite page: Here, a double border of Darwin hybrid tulips follows the curve of a driveway.

NATURALIZING

*Agapanthus	Hemerocallis
*Alstroemeria	Hyacinthoides
Anemone blanda	Iris cristata
Camassia	Lilium
Chionodoxa	*Lycoris
Colchicum	Muscari
Convallaria	Ornithogalum
*Crinum	Oxalis
Crocus	Scilla
Cyclamen	Tulipa species
Eranthis	*Zantedeschia
Erythronium	*Zephyranthes
Galanthus	

GROUND COVER

*Agapanthus	Hemerocallis
Convallaria	Iris cristata
Cyclamen	Oxalis

CUT FLOWERS

*Acidanthera	*Ixia
Agapanthus	Lilium
Allium	Narcissus
*Alstroemeria	*Ranunculus
*Crocosmia	Tigridia
Dahlia	Tulipa
*Eremurus	*Veltheimia
Gladiolus	*Watsonia
Iris	*Zantedeschia

DRIED ARRANGEMENTS

Allium giganteum
Belamcanda

ROADSIDE

*Agapanthus	Narcissus
Hemerocallis	Ornithogalum umbellatum
Iris pseudacorus	Oxalis
*Lycoris	Zephyranthes

SEASIDE GARDENS

*Agapanathus	Ixia
*Amaryllis	Lycoris
*Anemone coronaria	*Nerine
*Crinum	*Ranunculus
Gladiolus	*Veltheimia
*Hippeastrum	*Zantedeschia
*Hymenocallis	*Zephyranthes grandiflora
Iris	

FORCING

*Agapanthus
*Amaryllis
*Begonia
*Bletilla
*Caladium
*Clivia
Convallaria
Crocus
Cyclamen
Eranthis
*Eucharis
*Eucomis
Galanthus
*Gloriosa

*Haemanthus
*Hippeastrum
Hyacinthus
Iris
Lilium
Narcissus
*Nerine
*Pleione
*Ranunculus
*Scilla peruviana
*Sprekelia
Tulipa
*Veltheimia
*Zantedeschia

BULBS FOR FRAGRANCE

*Acidanthera
Convallaria
*Freesia
Hyacinthoides
Hyacinthus

Iris germanica
Lilium longiflorum
Narcissus
*Polianthes

BULBS ACCORDING TO HEIGHT

DWARF HABIT (1 FOOT OR LESS)

Allium karataviense
Allium moly
Anemone blanda
Babiana
Chionodoxa luciliae
Colchicum autumnale
Convallaria majalis
Crocus species
Cyclamen species
Eranthis hyemalis
Erythronium 'Pagoda'
Eucharis grandiflora
Fritillaria meleagris
Galanthus elwesii
Iris cristata
Iris danfordiae

Iris reticulata
Leucojum vernum
Muscari armeniacum
Narcissus species
   and hybrids
Ornithogalum thryrsoides
Ornithogalum umbellatum
Pleione formosa
Puschkinina scilloides
Ranunculus asiaticus
Scilla campanulata
Scilla siberica
Sinningia speciosa
Sternbergia lutea
Tulipa species
Zephyranthes atamasco

MEDIUM HEIGHT (1 TO 3 FEET)

Acidanthera bicolor
Allium christophii
Alstroemeria aurantiaca
Amaryllis belladonna
Anemone coronaria
Begonia tuberosa
Bletilla striata
Caladium hortulanum
Camassia esculenta
Clivia miniata
Crinum powelli
Dahlia pinnata
Freesia hybrida
Haemanthus katharinae
Hymenocallis narcissiflora

Iris hollandica
Ixia maculata
Leucojum aestivum
Lilium Asiatic hybrids
Lycoris radiata
Narcissus
Nerine bowdenii
Sparaxis tricolor
Sprekelia formosissima
Tigridia pavonia
Tulbaghia violacea
Tulip hybrids
Veltheimia viridifolia
Zantedeschia aethiopica

Opposite page: A simple, early-flowering bulb border featuring King Alfred daffodils, Red Emperor tulips, and a mixture of Dutch hyacinths.

TALL HABIT (3 FEET OR MORE)

Agapanthus africanus
Allium giganteum
Alstroemeria aurantiaca
Belamcanda chinensis
Canna generalis
Cardiocrinum giganteum
Colocasia esculenta
Dahlia pinnata
Eremurus elwesii
Fritillaria imperialis

Gladiolus hortulanus
Gloriosa rothschildiana
Hemerocallis fulva
Iris germanica
Iris kaempferi
Lilium
Lycoris squamigera
Polianthes tuberosa
Watsonia pyramidata

COLOR GUIDE

The following lists group bulbs by color. Asterisked varieties are tender:

WHITE

*Acidanthera
*Agapanthus
*Amaryllis
Anemone blanda
*Anemone coronaria
*Begonia
*Caladium
*Cardiocrinum
Convallaria
*Crinum
Crocus
Cyclamen
*Dahlia
*Eremurus
*Eucharis
*Erythronium
Fritillaria
Galanthus
*Gladiolus
*Hippeastrum
Hyacinthoides
Hyacinthus

*Hymenocallis
Iris
*Ixia
Leucojum
Lilium
Muscari
Narcissus
*Nerine
Ornithogalum
Pleione
*Polianthes
Puschkinia
Ranunculus
Scilla
*Sinningia
*Sparaxis
*Tigridia
Tritelia
Tulipa
*Watsonia
*Zantedeschia
*Zephyranthes

PURPLE

Allium
Anemone blanda
*Anemone coronaria
*Bletilla
Colchicum
Crocus
Dahlia
Fritillaria
*Gladiolus

Hemerocallis
Hyacinthus
Iris
*Nerine
*Pleione
*Sinningia
*Tulbaghia
Tulipa

BLUE
*Agapanthus
Anemone blanda
*Camassia
Chionodoxa
Crocus
Hyacinthoides

Hyacinthus
Iris
Muscari
Scilla
Tritelia

YELLOW-ORANGE
Allium moly
*Alstroemeria
Belamcanda
*Begonia
*Canna
*Clivia
Crocus
Dahlia
Eranthis
*Eremurus
Erythronium
*Eucomis
Fritillaria imperialis

*Gladiolus
Hemerocallis
Iris
*Ixia
Lilium
Narcissus
Oxalis
*Ranunculus
*Sparaxis
Sternbergia
Tulipa
*Zantedeschia
*Zephyranthes

RED/PINK
Alstroemeria
*Amaryllis
*Anemone coronaria
*Begonia
*Caladium
*Crinum
*Crocosmia
Cyclamen
*Dahlia
*Gladiolus
*Gloriosa
*Haemanthus
Hemerocallis
*Hippeastrum
Hyacinthus
*Incarvillea

Iris
*Ixia
Lilium
Lycoris
*Nerine
Oxalis
*Sinningia
*Sparaxis
*Sprekelia
Tulipa
*Veltheimia
*Watsonia
*Zantedeschia
*Zephyranthes

BULB PLANTING CHARTS

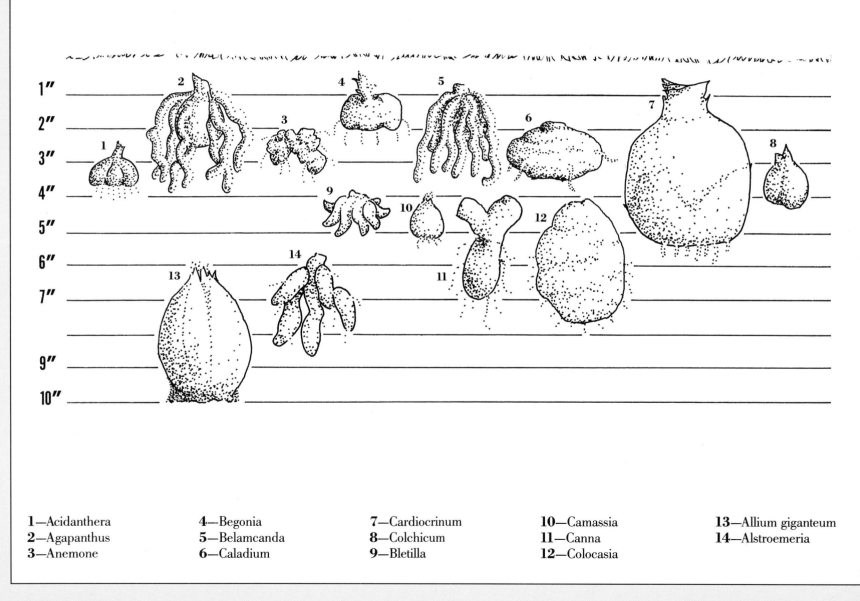

1—Acidanthera	**4**—Begonia	**7**—Cardiocrinum	**10**—Camassia	**13**—Allium giganteum
2—Agapanthus	**5**—Belamcanda	**8**—Colchicum	**11**—Canna	**14**—Alstroemeria
3—Anemone	**6**—Caladium	**9**—Bletilla	**12**—Colocasia	

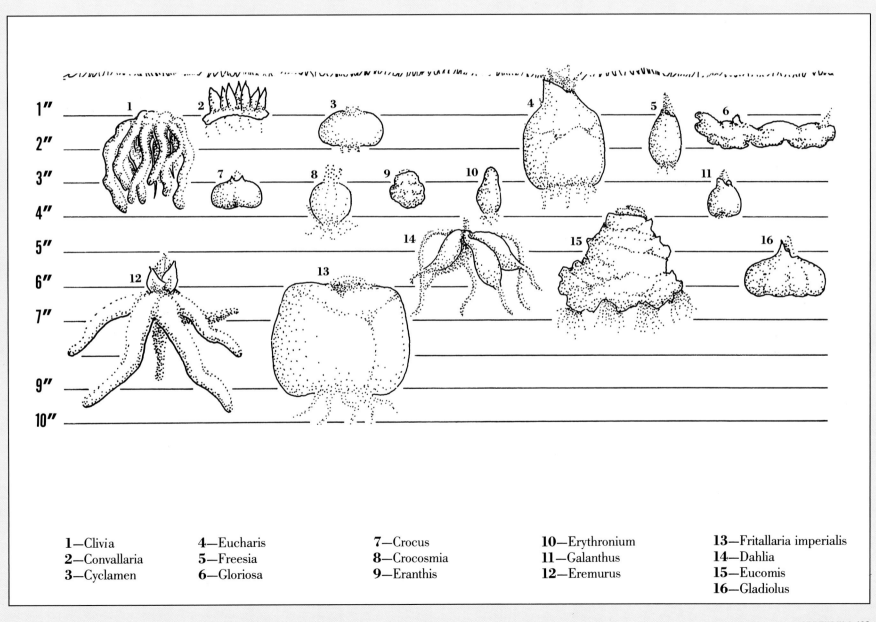

1″
2″
3″
4″
5″
6″
7″
9″
10″

1—Clivia 4—Eucharis 7—Crocus 10—Erythronium 13—Fritallaria imperialis
2—Convallaria 5—Freesia 8—Crocosmia 11—Galanthus 14—Dahlia
3—Cyclamen 6—Gloriosa 9—Eranthis 12—Eremurus 15—Eucomis
                                                      16—Gladiolus

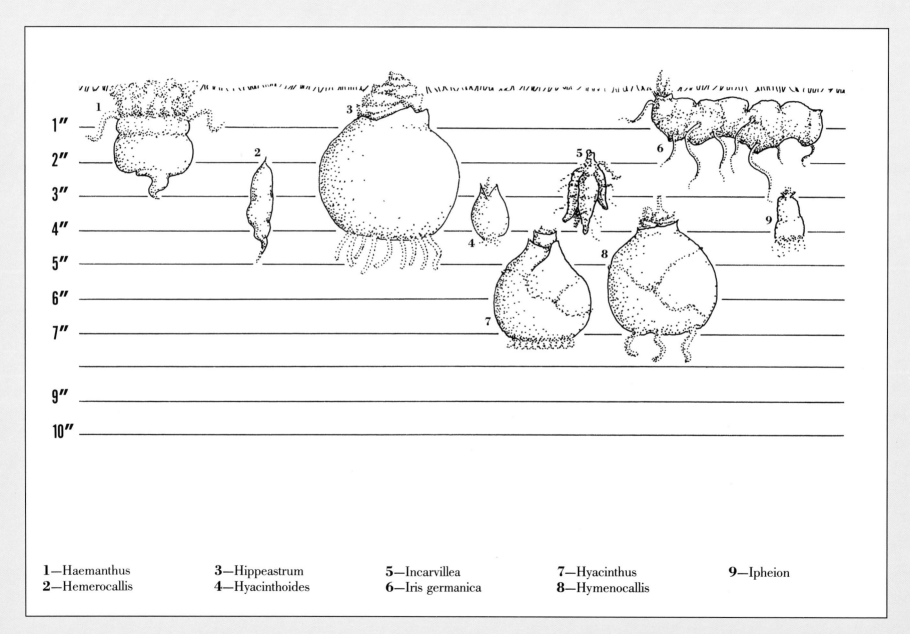

1—Haemanthus   3—Hippeastrum   5—Incarvillea   7—Hyacinthus   9—Ipheion
2—Hemerocallis   4—Hyacinthoides   6—Iris germanica   8—Hymenocallis

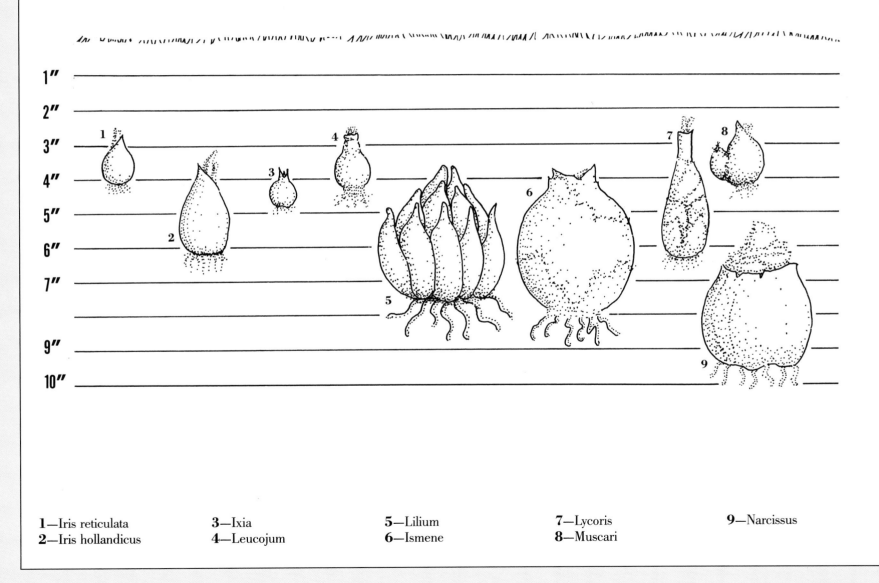

1"
2"
3"
4"
5"
6"
7"
9"
10"

1—Iris reticulata   **3**—Ixia   **5**—Lilium   **7**—Lycoris   **9**—Narcissus
2—Iris hollandicus   **4**—Leucojum   **6**—Ismene   **8**—Muscari

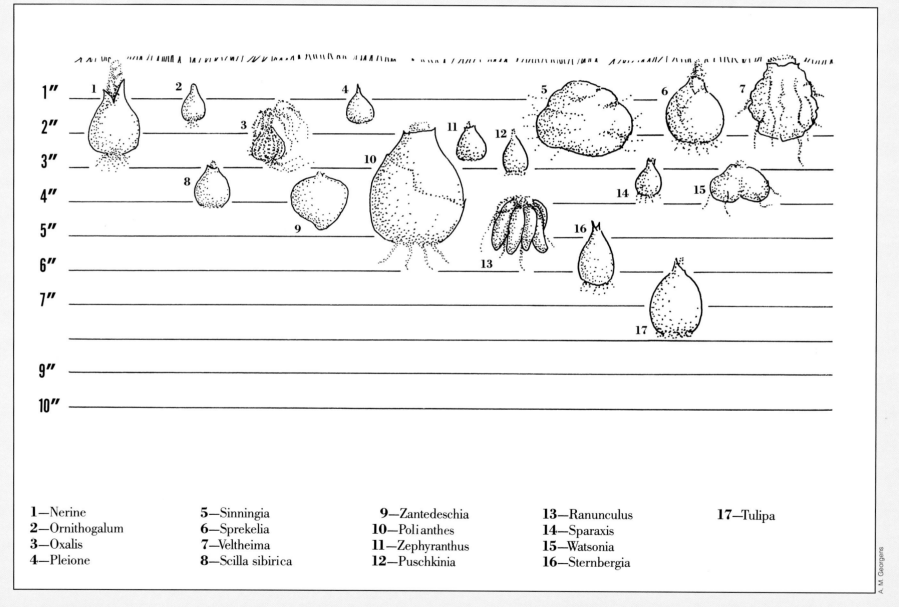

1"

2"

3"

4"

5"

6"

7"

9"

10"

1—Nerine
2—Ornithogalum
3—Oxalis
4—Pleione

5—Sinningia
6—Sprekelia
7—Veltheima
8—Scilla sibirica

9—Zantedeschia
10—Poli anthes
11—Zephyranthus
12—Puschkinia

13—Ranunculus
14—Sparaxis
15—Watsonia
16—Sternbergia

17—Tulipa

A. M. Georgens

Here, mixed tulips border a grassy walkway, adding brilliant color to this bulb garden.

BULB FLOWERING GUIDE

ZONE 1	BELOW -50°F
ZONE 2	-50° to -40°
ZONE 3	-40° to -30°
ZONE 4	-30° to -20°
ZONE 5	-20° to -10°
ZONE 6	-10° to -0°
ZONE 7	0 to 10°
ZONE 8	10° to 20°
ZONE 9	20° to 30°
ZONE 10	30° to 40°

BULB FLOWERING GUIDE

		Jan	Feb	Mar	Apr	May	Jun	Jul	Aug	Sep	Oct	Nov	Dec
Acidanthera bicolor	(Peacock Flower)							█	█				
Agapanthus africanus	(African Lily)					█	█	█					
Allium christophii	(Star-of-Persia)					█	█						
Allium giganteum	(Giant Allium)						█						
Allium moly	(Lily Leek)				█	█							
Allium schoenoprasum	(Chive)					█							
Alstroemeria aurantiaca	(Peruvian Lily)							█					
Amaryllis belladonna	(Naked Ladies, Belladonna Lily)										█		
Anemone blanda	(Grecian Windflower)				█								
Anemone coronaria	(French Anemone)												
Begonia x *tuberhybrida*	(Tuberous Begonia)						█	█	█	█			
Belamcanda chinensis	(Blackberry-Lily)						█	█					
Bletilla striata	(Chinese Orchid)				█	█							
Caladium x *hortulanum*	(Rainbow Plant)						█	█	█	█			
Camassia scilloides	(Wild Hyacinth)				█	█							
Canna x *generalis*	(Canna)							█	█	█			
Cardiocrinum giganteum	(Himalayan Lily)						█						
Chionodoxa luciliae	(Glory-of-the-Snow)				█	█							
Clivia miniata	(Kafir-Lily)				█								
Colchicum autumnale	(Autumn-Crocus)									█			
Colocasia esculenta	(Elephant's Ear, Giant Taro)							█	█	█			
Convallaria majalis	(Lily-of-the-valley)					█							
Crocosmia x *crocosmiiflora*	(Montbretia)							█	█				

		January	February	March	April	May	June	July	August	September	October	November	December
Crocus chrysanthus	(Snow Crocus)				■								
Crocus flavus	(Yellow Crocus)										■		
Crocus tomasinianus	(Common Crocus)			■	■								
Cyclamen neapolitanum	(Hardy Cyclamen)				■	■							
Cyclamen persicum	(Florists' Cyclamen)	■	■									■	■
Dahlia pinnata hybrids	(Dahlia)						■	■	■	■			
Eranthis hyemalis	(Winter Aconite)		■	■									
Eremurus elwesii	(Foxtail Lily)					■	■						
Erythronium 'Pagoda'	(Dogtooth Violet)				■								
Eucharis grandiflora	(Amazon-Lily)			■									
Eucomis comosa	(Pineapple Lily)							■	■	■			
Freesia x *hybrida*	(Freesia)					■							
Fritillaria imperialis	(Crown Imperial)				■	■							
Fritillaria meleagris	(Checkered Lily)				■								
Galanthus elwesii	(Snowdrop)		■	■									
Gladiolus x *hortulanus*	(Gladiolus)							■	■	■			
Gloriosa rothschildiana	(Rothschild Gloriosa-Lily)				■	■				■	■		
Haemanthus katharinae	(Katharine Blood-Lily)						■						
Hemerocallis fulva	(Tawny Daylily)						■	■	■				
Hippeastrum hybrida	(Amaryllis)		■	■	■	■							
Hyacinthus orientalis	(Dutch Hyacinth)				■								
Hyacinthoides hispanica	(Spanish Bluebell)					■							
Hymenocallis narcissiflora	(Peruvian Daffodil)					■							

		January	February	March	April	May	June	July	August	September	October	November	December
Hyacinthoides hispanica	(Spanish Bluebells)					■							
Hymenocallis narcissiflora	(Peruvian Daffodil)					■							
Incarvillea delvayii	(Hardy Gloxinia)					■	■						
Iris cristata	(Crested Iris)					■							
Iris danfordiae	(Danford Iris)			■									
Iris x *germanica*	(Bearded Iris)						■						
Ixia maculata	(Corn-Lily)				■								
Leucojum vernum	(Spring Snowflake)				■								
Lilium auratum	(Oriental Lily)								■				
Lilium candidum	(Madonna Lily, Bermuda Lily)							■					
Lilium hybrida 'asiatic'	(Asiatic Hybrid Lilies)							■					
Lilium longiflorum	(White Trumpet Lily)								■	■			
Lilium superbum	(Turkscap Lily)								■				
Lycoris radiata	(Red Spider Lily)									■			
Lycoris squamigera	(Naked Ladies)									■			
Muscari armeniacum	(Grape hyacinth)				■								
Narcissus poeticus	(Poet's Daffodil)				■								
Narcissus triandrus	(Daffodil, Angels Tears)				■								
Ornithogalum umbellatum	(Star of Bethlehem)					■							
Oxalis pes-caprae	(Bermuda Buttercup)				■								
Pleione formosa	(Fairy Orchid)				■								
Polianthes x *tuberosa*	(Tuberose)									■			
Puschkinia scilloides	(Striped Squill)					■	■						

		January	February	March	April	May	June	July	August	September	October	November	December
Scilla siberica	(Siberian squill)				▓								
Sinningia speciosa	(Gloxinia)						▓	▓					
Sparaxis tricolor	(Harlequin flower)				▓								
Sprekelia formosissima	(Jakobean Lily)					▓							
Sternbergia lutea	(Fall Crocus)									▓			
Tigrida pavonia	(Tiger-Flowers, Shell-Flowers)							▓	▓				
Triteleia uniflora	(Star Flower)				▓	▓							
Tulbaghia violacea	(Society Garlic)					▓	▓						
Tulipa clusiana	(Candlestick Tulip, Peppermint Stick)				▓								
Tulipa dasystemon	(Tulip)				▓								
Tulipa fosteriana	(Foster Tulip)				▓								
Tulipa greigii	(Peacock Tulip)				▓								
Tulipa x *hybrida* 'Darwin'	(Darwin Hybrid Tulip)				▓								
Tulipa x *hybrida* 'Lily-Flowered'	(Lily-Flowered Tulip)				▓								
Tulipa kaufmanniana	(Water-Lily Tulip)				▓								
Tulipa x *hybrida* 'Parrot'	(Parrot-Flowered Tulip)				▓	▓							
Tulipa x *hybrida* 'Peony-Flowered'	(Peony-Flowered Tulip)				▓	▓							
Tulipa praestans	(Leather-Bulb Tulip)				▓								
Veltheimia viridifolia	(Cape Lily)												
Watsonia pyramidata	(Bugle Flower)							▓					
Zantedeschia aethiopica	(Calla Lily)					▓							
Zephyranthes atamasco	(Atamasco Lily, Zephyr Lily)				▓								

Mixed tulip colors and grape hyacinths make a beautiful bed, brightening the view from this window.

SOURCES

SPRING- AND SUMMER- BLOOMING BULBS

BAKKER OF HOLLAND
Box 50
Louisiana, MO 63353
Catalog free

BRECKS
Box 1757
Peoria, IL 61656
Catalog free

BURPEE BULBS
300 Park Avenue
Warminster, PA 18974
Catalog free

PETER DE JAGER BULB CO.
Box 2010
South Hamilton, MA 01982
Catalog free

DUTCH GARDENS
Box 200
Adelphia, NJ 07710
Catalog $1.00

GURNEY SEED & NURSERY
Second & Capital Streets
Yankton, SD 57078
Catalog free

INTERNATIONAL GROWERS
   EXCHANGE
Box 52248
Livonia, MI 48152
Catalog $5.00

J.W. JUNG CO.
335 S. High Street
Randolph, WI 53957
Catalog free

EARL MAY NURSERY CO.
Box 500
Shenandoah, IA 51603
Catalog free

MESSELAAR BULB CO.
Box 269
Ipswich, MA 01938
Catalog free

MICHIGAN BULB CO.
1950 Waldorf NW
Grand Rapids, MI 49550
Catalog free

PARK SEED COMPANY
Box 46
Greenwood, SC 29648
Catalog free

PINETREE GARDEN SEEDS
Rte. 100N
Gloucester, ME 04260
Catalog free

JOHN SCHEEPERS INC.
63 Wall Street
New York, NY 10005
Catalog free

TY TY PLANTATION
Box 159
Ty Ty, Ga 31795
Catalog free

K. VAN BOURGANDIEN & SONS,
   INC.
Box A
Babylon, NY 11702
Catalog free

VAN ENGELEN, INC.
307 Maple Street
Litchfield, CT 06759
Catalog free

WAUSHARA GARDENS
Box 570
Plainfield, WI 54966
Catalog $1.00

WAYSIDE GARDENS
Box 1
Hodges, SC 29695
Catalog $1.00

WHITE FLOWER FARM
Rte. 63
Litchfield, CT 06759
Catalog $5.00

SPECIALTIES

AMARYLLIS (HIPPEASTRUM)

AMARYLLIS INC.
Box 318
Baton Rouge, LA 78021
Catalog $1.00

BEGONIAS

ANTONELLI BROTHERS
2545 Capitol Road
Santa Cruz, CA 95062
Catalog $1.00

FAIRYLAND BEGONIA GARDEN
1100 Griffith Road
McKinleyville, CA 95521
Catalog 50¢

KARTUZ GREENHOUSES
1408 Sunset Drive
Vista, CA 92083
Catalog $2.00

DAHLIAS

BLUE DAHLIA GARDENS
Box 316
San Jose, IL 62682
Catalog free

CONNELL'S DAHLIAS
10216 40th Avenue
Tacoma, WA 98446
Catalog $1.00

DAHLIAS BY PHIL TRAFF
1316 132nd Avenue
Summer, WA 98390
Catalog free

LEGG DAHLIA GARDENS
1069 Hastings Road
Geneva, NY 14456
Catalog free

SWAN ISLAND DAHLIAS
Box 800
Canby, OR 97013
Catalog $2.00

GLADIOLUS

FLAD'S GLADS
2109 Cliff Court
Madison, WI 53713
Catalog $1.00

GLADSIDE GARDENS
61 Main Street
Northfield, MA 01360
Catalog $1.00

HEMEROCALLIS (DAYLILIES)

AMERICAN DAYLILY &
  PERENNIALS
Box 7008
The Woodlands, TX 77380
Catalog $3.00

DAYLILY WORLD
Box 1612
Sanford, FL 32771
Catalog free

GREENWOOD NURSERY
Box 1610
Goleta, Ca 93116
Catalog $3.00

KLEHM NURSERY
Box 197
South Barrington, IL 60010
Catalog $2.00

GILBERT H. WILD & SON, INC.
P. O. Box 338
1112 Joplin Street
Sarcoxie, MO 64862
Catalog $2.00

IRIS

COMANCHE ACRES
  IRIS GARDENS
Box 258
Gower, MO 64454
Catalog $1.00

COOLEY'S GARDENS
Box 126
11553 Silverton Road, NE
Silverton, OR 97381
Catalog $2.00

FRENCH IRISH GARDENS
621 S. 3rd Avenue
Walla Walla, WA 99362
Catalog $2.00

GARDEN OF THE ENCHANTED
  RAINBOW
Box 439
Killeen, AL 35645
Catalog $1.00

MAPLE TREE GARDENS
Box 278
Ponca, NE 68770
Catalog free

McMILLENS IRIS GARDEN
R. R. #1
Norwich, ONT Canada, NOJ 1PO
Catalog free

SHREINERS GARDENS
3625 Quinaby Road NE
Salem, OR 97303
Catalog $2.00

LILIUM

OREGON BULB FARMS
14071 N.E. Arndt Road
Aurora, OR 97002
Catalog $2.00

REX BULB FARMS
Box 774
Port Townsend, WA 98368
Catalog free

NARCISSUS

THE DAFFODIL MART
Box 794
Gloucester, VA 23061
Catalog free

GRANT MITSCH NOVELTY
  DAFFODILS
Box 218
Hubbard, OR 97032
Catalog $3.00

CHARLES H. MUELLER
River Road
New Hope, PA. 18938
Catalog free

OAKWOOD DAFFODILS
2330 W. Bertrand Road
Niles, MI 49120
Catalog free

TULIPS

VELDHEER TULIP GARDENS
12755 Quincy Street
Holland, MI 49424
Catalog free

Index Of Botanical And Common Names

A

Acidanthera bicolor, 26
Aconite. *See Eranthis hyemalis*
African Lily. *See Agapanthus africanus*
Agapanthus africanus, 26
Allium christophii, 27
Allium giganteum, 27
Allium moly, 28
Allium schoenoprasum, 28
Alstroemeria aurantiaca, 29
Amaryllis. *See Crinum x powellii; Hippeastrum hybrida*
Amaryllis belladonna, 29
Amazon-Lily. *See Eucharis grandiflora*
Anemone blanda, 30
Anemone coronaria, 30
Angels Tears. *See Narcissus triandrus*
Asiatic Hybrid Lilies. *See Lilium hybrida asiatic*
Atamasco Lily. *See Zephyranthes atamasco*
Autumn-Crocus. *See Colchicum autumnale*

B

Babiana stricta, 31
Baboon Flower. *See Babiana stricta*
Bearded Iris. *See Iris x germanica*
Begonia. *See Begonia x tuberhybrida*
Begonia x tuberhybrida, 31
Belamcanda chinensis, 33
Belladonna Lily. *See Amaryllis belladonna*

Bermuda Buttercup. *See Oxalis pres-caprae*
Bermuda Lily. *See Lilium candidum*
Blackberry-Lily. *See Belamcanda chinensis*
Bletilla striata, 33
Blood-Lily. *See Haemanthus katharinae*
Bugle Flower. *See Watsonia pyramidata*
Bulbs
    colors of, 124-25
    for cut flowers, 120
    for dried arrangements, 120
    dwarf, 123
    fall colors, 118
    fertilizing of, 22
    forcing, 123
    for fragrance, 123
    for ground cover, 120
    hardy types, 117
    height of, 123-24
    history of growing, 10-11
    indoor growth of, 18-21
    medium height, 123
    moisture tolerant, 119
    naturalizing, 120
    outdoor growth of, 21-23
    planting time for, 13-14
    potting of, 19-20
    protection from pests and diseases, 23
    roadside, 120
    for seaside gardens, 120
    shade tolerant, 119
    spring-flowering, 14-18, 119

    summer-flowering, 118-19
    tall height, 124
    tender types, 117
    types defined, 13
    windowsill flowering of, 20
Buttercup. *See Oxalis pes-caprae; Ranunculus asiaticus*

C

Caladium x hortulanum, 34
Calla Lily. *See Zantedeschia aethiopica*
Camassia scilloides, 34
Candlestick Tulip. *See Tulipa clusiana*
Canna. *See Canna x generalis*
Canna x generalis, 36
Cape Lily. *See Veltheimia viridifolia*
Cardiocrinum giganteum, 36
Carolus Clusias, 10
Checkered Lily. *See Fritillaria meleagris*
Chincherinchee. *See Ornithogalum thyrsoides*
Chinese Orchid. *See Bletilla striata*
Chionodoxa luciliae, 37
Chives. *See Allium schoenoprasum*
Clivia miniata, 37
Colchicum autumnale, 38
Colocasia esculenta, 38
Common Crocus. *See Crocus vernus*
Convallaria majalis, 39
Corms, 13
Corn-Lily. *See Ixia maculata*
Crested Iris. *See Iris cristata*

Crinum x powellii, 39
Crocosmia x crocosmiiflora, 41
Crocus. *See Colchicum autumnale; Crocus chrysanthus; Crocus flavus; Crocus tomasinianus; Crocus vernus; Sternbergia lutea*
Crocus chrysanthus, 41
Crocus flavus, 42
Crocus tomasinianus, 42
Crocus vernus, 44
Crown Imperial. *See Fritillaria imperialis*
Cyclamen. *See Cyclamen hederifolium; Cyclamen persicum*
Cyclamen hederifolium, 44
Cyclamen persicum, 45

D

Daffodil. *See Hymenocallis narcissiflora; Narcissus minimum; Narcissus poeticus; Narcissus triandrus; Narcissus triandrus; Narcissus x hybrida* 'Double-Flowered'; *Narcissus x hybrida* 'Trumpet-Flowered'
Dahlia. *See Dahlia pinnata hybrids*
Dahlia pinnata hybrids, 45
Danford Iris. *See Iris danfordiae*
Darwin Hybrid Tulips. *See Tulipa x hybrida* 'Darwin'
Dioscorides, 10
Dogtooth Violet. *See Erythronium* 'Pagoda'
Double-Flowered Daffodil. *See Narcissus x*

hybrida 'Double-flowered'
du Pont, Henry F., 9
Dutch Crocus. *See Crocus vernus*
Dutch Hyacinth. *See Hyacinthus orientalis*
Dutch Iris. *See Iris hollandica*
Dwarf Blue Iris. *See Iris reticulata*

E

Elephant's Ear. *See Colocasia esculenta*
Eranthis hyemalis, 46
Eremurus elwesii, 46
Erythronium 'Pagoda', 47
Eucharis grandiflora, 47
Eucomis comosa, 49

F

Fairy Orchid. *See Pleione formosa*
Fall Crocus. *See Sternbergia lutea*
Florists' Cyclamen. *See Cyclamen persicum*
Foster Tulip. *See Tulipa fosterana*
Foxtail Lily. *See Eremurus elwesii*
Freesia. *See Freesia x hybrida*
Freesia x hybrida, 49
French Anemone. *See Anemone coronaria*
Fritillaria imperialis, 50
Fritillaria meleagris, 50

G

Galanthus elwesii, 52
Giant Allium. *See Allium giganteum*
Giant Taro. *See Colocasia esculenta*

Gladiolus. *See Gladiolus x hortulanus*
Gladiolus x hortulanus, 52
Gloriosa rothschildiana, 53
Gloriosa-Lily. *See Gloriosa rothschildiana*
Glory-of-the-Snow. *See Chionodoxa luciliae*
Gloxinia. *See Incarvillea delvayii; Sinningia speciosa*
Golden Crocus. *See Crocus chrysanthus*
Grape Hyacinth. *See Muscari armeniacum*
Grecian Windflower. *See Anemone blanda*

H

Haemanthus katharinae, 53
Hardy Cyclamen. *See Cyclamen hederifolium*
Hardy Gloxinia. *See Incarvillea delvayii*
Harlequin Flower. *See Sparaxis tricolor*
Hemerocallis fulva, 54
Himalayan Lily. *See Cardiocrinum giganteum*
Hippeastrum hybrida, 54
History of Plants and Theoretical Botany, A (Theophrastus), 10
Holland, tulip cultivation in, 10-11
Hortus Medicus garden (Leyden), 10
Hyacinth. *See Camassia scilloides; Hyacinthus orientalis; Muscari armeniacum*
Hyacinthoides hispanica, 55
Hyacinthus orientalis, 55
Hymenocallis narcissiflora, 57

I

Incarvillea delvayii, 57

Iris. *See Iris cristata; Iris danfordiae; Iris hollandica; Iris kaempferi; Iris reticulata; Iris x germanica*
Iris cristata, 58
Iris danfordiae, 58
Iris x germanica, 60
Iris hollandica, 60
Iris kaempferi, 61
Iris reticulata, 61
Ismene. *See Hymenocallis narcissflora*
Ixia maculata, 62

J

Jacobean-Lily. *See Sprekelia formosissima*
Japanese Iris. *See Iris kaempferi*

K

Kafir-Lily. *See Clivia miniata*
Keukenhoff garden (Holland), 9
Kuenlun Tulip. *See Tulipa dasystemon*

L

Leaf mold, 22
Leather-Bulb Tulip. *See Tulipa praestans*
Leucojum vernum, 62
Lilium auratum, 63
Lilium candidum, 63
Lilium hybrida asiatic, 65
Lilium longiflorum, 65
Lilium superbum, 66

Lily. *See Agapanthus africanus; Alstroemeria aurantiaca; Amaryllis belladonna; Belamcanda chinensis; Cardiocrinum giganteum; Clivia miniata; Eremurus elwesii; Eucharis grandiflora; Eucomis comosa; Fritillaria meleagris; Gloriosa rothschildiana; Haemanthus katharinae; Ixia maculata; Lilium auratum; Lilium candidum; Lilium hybrida asiatic; Lilium longiflorum; Lilium superbum; Lycoris radiata; Sprekelia formosissima; Veltheimia viridifolia; Zantedeschia aethiopica; Zephyranthes atamasco*
Lily Leek. *See Allium moly*
Lily-Flowered Tulip. *See Tulipa x hybrida 'Lily-Flowered'*
Lily-of-the-Nile. *See Agapanthus africanus*
Lily-of-the-Valley. *See Convallaria majalis*
Lycoris radiata, 66
Lycoris squamigera, 68

M

Madonna Lily. *See Lilium candidum*
Medicinal use of bulbs, 10
Minature Daffodil. *See Narcissus minimum*
Montbretia. *See Crocosmia x crocosmiiflora*
Muscari armeniacum, 68

N

Naked Ladies. *See Amaryllis belladonna; Lycoris squamigera*

Narcissus minimum, 70
Narcissus poeticus, 70
Narcissus triandrus, 71
Narcissus x *hybrida* 'Double-flowered', 69
Narcissus x *hybrida* 'Trumpet-flowered', 69
Nerine. *See Nerine bowdenii*
Nerine bowdenii, 71

O

Orchid. *See Bletilla striata; Pleione
    formosa*
Oriental Lily. *See Lilium auratum*
Ornithogalum thyrsoides, 73
Ornithogalum umbellatum, 73
Oxalis pes-caprae, 74

P

Parrot-Flowered Tulip. *See Tulipa* x *hybrida*
    '*Parrot*'
Peacock Flower. *See Acidanthera bicolor*
Peacock Tulip. *See Tulipa greigii*
Peony-Flowered Tulip. *See Tulipa* x *hybrida*
    '*Peony-Flowered*'
Peppermint Stick. *See Tulipa clusiana*
Persian Buttercup. *See Ranunculus asiaticus*
Peruvian Daffodil. *See Hymenocallis
    narcissflora*
Peruvian Lily. *See Alstroemeria aurantiaca*
Peruvian Squill. *See Scilla peruviana*
Pheasant's Eye. *See Narcissus poeticus*
Pineapple Lily. *See Eucomis comosa*

Planting times, 13-14
Pleione formosa, 74
Pliny, 10
Poet's Daffodil. *See Narcissus poeticus*
Polianthes x *tuberosa*, 76
Poppy Anemone. *See Anemone coronaria*
Puschkinia scilloides, 76

R

Rainbow Plant. *See Caladium* x *hortulanum*
Ranunculus asiaticus, 77
Red Spider Lily. *See Lycoris radiata*
Rhizomes, 13

S

Scilla campanulata, 77
Scilla peruviana, 78
Scilla sibirica, 78
Shell-flowers. *See Tigridia pavonia*
Siberian Squill. *See Scilla sibirica*
Sinningia speciosa, 79
Snow Crocus. *See Crocus tomasinianus*
Snowdrop. *See Galanthus elwesii*
Society Garlic. *See Tulbaghia violacea*
Soil, 14
Soil conditioning, 23
Spanish Bluebell. *See Hyacinthoides
    hispanica; Scilla campanulata*
Sparaxis tricolor, 79
Sprekelia formosissima, 81
Spring Snowflake. *See Leucojum vernum*

Squill. *See Puschkinia scilloides; Scilla
    peruviana; Scilla sibirica*
Star of Bethlehem. *See Ornithogalum
    umbellatum*
Starflower. *See Triteleia uniflora*
Star-of-Persia. *See Allium christophii*
Sternbergia lutea, 81
Striped Squill. *See Puschkinia scilloides*
Summer Amaryllis. *See Crinum* x *powellii*

T

Tawny Daylily. *See Hemerocallis fulva*
Theophrastus, 10
Tiger-Flowers. *See Tigridia pavonia*
Tigridia pavonia, 82
Triteleia uniflora, 82
True bulbs, 13
Trumpet Daffodil. *See Narcissus* x *hybrida*
    '*Trumpet-flowered*'
Tuberose. *See Polyanthus* x *tuberosa*
Tuberous Begonia. *See Begonia* x
    tuberhybrida
Tubers, 13
Tulbaghia violacea, 84
Tulip. *See Tulipa clusiana; Tulipa
    dasystemon; Tulipa fosterana; Tulipa
    greigii; Tulipa kaufmanniana; Tulipa
    praestans; Tulipa* x *hybrida* '*Darwin*';
    Tulipa x *hybrida* '*Lily-Flowered*'; *Tulipa*
    x *hybrida* '*Parrot*'; *Tulipa* x *hybrida*
    '*Peony-Flowered*'

Tulipa clusiana, 84
Tulipa dasystemon, 85
Tulipa fosterana, 85
Tulipa greigii, 86
Tulipa x *hybrida* '*Darwin*', 86
Tulipa x *hybrida* '*Lily-Flowered*', 87
Tulipa x *hybrida* '*Parrot*', 87
Tulipa x *hybrida* '*Peony-Flowered*', 89
Tulipa kaufmanniana, 89
Tulipa praestans, 90
Turkscap Lily. *See Lilium superbum*

V

Veltheimia viridifolia, 90
Violet. *See Erythronium* '*Pagoda*'

W

Water-Lily Tulip. *See Tulipa kaufmanniana*
Watsonia pyramidata, 92
White Trumpet Lily. *See Lilium longiflorum*
Wild Hyacinth. *See Camassia scilloides*
Winter Aconite. *See Eranthis hyemalis*
Winterthur garden (Delaware), 9

Y

Yellow Crocus. *See Crocus flavus*

Z

Zantedeschia aethiopica, 92
Zephyr Lily. *See Zephyranthes atamasco*
Zephyranthes atamasco, 93